THE BOOK OF
NATIONAL TRUST
RECIPES

Sarah Edington

THE BOOK OF NATIONAL TRUST RECIPES

The National Trust

ISBN 0 7078 0092 7

Copyright © Sarah Edington 1988

First published in Great Britain in 1988
Reprinted May 1988, August 1988
by The National Trust,
36 Queen Anne's Gate,
London, SW1H 9AS

The illustrations of National Trust properties
are by Andrew Macdonald, Claude Page,
David Peacock and Eric Thomas. All other
illustrations are from *Forgotten Household
Crafts* by John Seymour, reproduced by kind
permission of Dorling Kindersley Ltd.

Designed by James Shurmer
Phototypeset in Monotype Lasercomp Garamond 156
by Southern Positives and Negatives (SPAN),
Lingfield, Surrey

Printed in England by The Bath Press, Avon

CONTENTS

CONTENTS *continued*

ACKNOWLEDGEMENTS

My thanks to all the cooks who gave me these recipes:

Pat Anscombe	Betty Jones
David Bainton	Dawn Jones
Doreen Beddows	Christine Kydd
Doreen Bond	Joan Mapperley
Anne Chamberlain	Barbara Mattey
Maureen Dodsworth	Gladys Middlemiss
Pat Fletcher	Theresa Owens
John Forrest	Phyl Parker
Jackie Fry	Linda Parsons
Sue Gadd	Mary Parsons
Sally Gray	Barbara Rhodes
Fred Groves	Chris Ritson
Fiona Harris	Wendy Scerri
Jacky Hazeldene	Gillian Short
Myrtle Helsdon	Maureen Smith
Clare Henderson	Jayne Spenceley
Margaret Holtby	Pauline Thomas
Margaret Hughes	Tam White
Carrol Jackson	Margaret Wilkes

I would also like to thank Esme Auer, who helped
me to write and type the recipes.

In memory of my mother
who made me a member of the National Trust,
and to John and the girls
who encouraged me and put up with the travelling.

FOREWORD

When people are asked what the National Trust is and does, a curious series of images tends to emerge – the chief of which suggests that it is a government body that looks after stately homes. Government body it is not, but a charity maintained by the subscriptions of its members. The Trust does indeed 'look after' well over 100 stately homes of varied size, shape and age, but it was originally set up as a conservation organisation to save areas of outstanding natural beauty. The Trust, moreover, has many other facets, and perhaps one of the least well known is its catering enterprise.

Legend has it that the Trust's catering activities began with a bun and a cup of tea served through the window of a gardener's cottage at Hidcote. In the 1970s new tea-shops and restaurants were opened in Trust properties throughout the country. Those in Cornwall and Devon soon became noted for their excellent home cooking and have featured in *The Good Food Guide*. Not to be outdone by efforts in the South West, the Trust's other fourteen regions in England, Wales and Northern Ireland have expanded their activities with great panache over the past ten years, producing a catering 'chain' of some significance: nearly 100 restaurants, cafés and tea-rooms, not forgetting the Trust's small hotel, the Spread Eagle at Stourhead.

Although expansion has been rapid, the Trust has striven constantly to maintain standards, quality and style. Dame Jennifer Jenkins, Chairman of the National Trust, recently summed this up: 'The Trust's philosophy has always been to concentrate on the sort of catering that we know we do well – homely dishes, prepared on the premises, using fresh ingredients, and with great emphasis on home baking, particularly those delicious scones and cakes. I believe this is sound policy which we shall continue, bringing in present-day tastes for lighter, weight-watcher dishes, vegetarian food and alcohol-free drinks. The Trust is actively supporting the revival of traditional British cooking and our wine lists feature a selection of English wines, or local cider and beer.'

Sarah Edington has for some years now organised catering for special occasions at the Trust's London headquarters, so that her culinary expertise makes her an exacting and searching judge of the Trust's restaurants and tea-rooms throughout the country. She has experienced green pea and mint soup in the mock Norman castle of Penrhyn in North Wales, beef layer pie with yoghurt topping amid the Baroque splendour of Beningbrough in Yorkshire, and chocolate éclairs under the formidable gaze of Bess at Hardwick Hall in Derbyshire. Her resulting selection, we hope, will provide a mouthwatering guide to the recipes of the National Trust. Try cooking them, then go and visit the houses and properties from whence they came and discover the Trust's manifold delights.

Martin Moss
Director of National Trust Enterprises

INTRODUCTION

I first thought of *The Book of National Trust Recipes* some time ago. I am a professional cook and I was asked to go down to Cotehele, a wonderful Cornish manor and estate (featured in this book) to organise and cook a buffet lunch for the opening of the Maritime Museum at Cotehele Quay on the banks of the River Tamar. I could use the kitchens at the house. Well, I packed my sharpest knives and my cleanest apron and arrived the day before the party on the hottest day of the year. Despite the steamy atmosphere, the pressure I was under and the need to share the kitchen, I started to get on famously with the formidable Cornish lady in charge once I spotted her delicious scones laid out ready for Cornish cream teas. I asked her for the recipe, difficulties melted away and I have been making the scones ever since.

It set me thinking – there must be a lot of good English food being produced efficiently and quietly at National Trust properties. What about a book, part souvenir, part recipe book, part encouragement to visitors? Fired with enthusiasm, I approached the National Trust and eventually all the details were settled and I was able to start contacting the cooks and visiting the properties.

I have had a wonderful time. There are recipes from 31 properties in this book and I have visited every one of them – elegant mansions, spectacular castles, intimate and enchanting houses, great gardens and estates. Before I set out I was worried that I would be overwhelmed by the mass of information, that I would be unable to remember each place clearly. I need not have worried. Each property is totally individual, and fascinating in its own particular way. I finished my travelling an even more devoted visitor than I began.

I was also delighted to find my hunch was right and that good English country cooking using locally available ingredients is alive and flourishing in the restaurants and tea-rooms attached to Trust properties. Many restaurants started by serving teas and still offer a wealth of cakes, scones, biscuits and teabreads, often using recipes with local associations, such as Shrewsbury biscuits, parkin and Eccles cakes. Many, too, make use of regional or unusual ingredients such as the carrot and banana cake from Hidcote and cider cakes from the West Country.

But many places now also provide lunches and there are recipes to suit both light and hearty appetites. Imaginative combinations in the sustaining soups on offer include Stilton and onion, celery and almond, and green pea and mint. You will find the traditional old English favourites such as shepherd's pie and steak and kidney pie, but also interesting new ideas. I was particularly taken with the beef layer pie with yoghurt topping.

Menus in National Trust restaurants also reflect the current interest in healthy eating and I was very excited to find so many unusual and inventive vegetarian recipes using all the new ingredients, spices and herbs that are now freely available in England. New, too, are the interesting salads – a far cry from limp lettuce and soggy beetroot. Combinations such as carrot and cashew, courgette and red pepper, fennel and cabbage provide healthy and tempting alternatives to a hot meal.

But one of the greatest delights of eating at a Trust restaurant is sampling the extensive range of that particularly English speciality: the pudding. Often wickedly fattening, or served with lashings of thick cream, many use the fruits for which English gardens are famous and are colourful as well as delicious. You will find recipes for over thirty different puddings here and all are irresistible.

Since these are mostly family recipes, quantities are also family size and will serve four to six people according to appetite. Where cakes are concerned, I have given a tin size. Some of the soups and salads were difficult to reduce to one-meal quantities and you may well find that they will feed another set of hungry mouths at another meal on the next day! Eggs are all standard size 3 unless otherwise indicated. If no sugar variety is given, use caster sugar. I have given cooking times and temperatures but find from personal experience that these do vary from oven to oven so do regard them more as an indication than an order. Where cakes and sponge puddings are concerned, for instance, the best test is to plunge a stainless-steel skewer into the centre of the cake or pudding – if this comes out clean, the cake or pudding is cooked. Most cakes should be taken out of their tins and cooled on a wire tray after cooking, and only stored after they are cold. Similarly, all biscuits should be cooled on a wire tray and put in a tin only after they are cold.

Last but not least, do go to the restaurants and tea-rooms and sample for yourselves all the other delicious recipes and dishes that there was no room to include here.

CONVERSIONS

The following approximate conversions are used in this book
American equivalents will be found on page 157

$\frac{1}{2}$oz	13g	7oz	200g
1oz	25g	8oz	225g
2oz	50g	12oz	350g
3oz	75g	1lb	450g
4oz	100g	1$\frac{1}{2}$lb	700g
5oz	125g	2lb	900g
6oz	175g		

$\frac{1}{4}$in	6mm	6in	15cm
$\frac{1}{2}$in	12mm	7in	18cm
$\frac{3}{4}$in	2cm	8in	20cm
1in	2.5cm	9in	23cm
1$\frac{1}{2}$in	4cm	10in	25cm
2in	5cm	12in	30cm

1 teaspoon	5ml	5 fluid oz	150ml
1 dessertspoon	10ml	6 fluid oz	180ml
1 tablespoon	15ml	12 fluid oz	360ml
1 fluid oz	30ml	15 fluid oz	450ml
4 fluid oz	120ml	20 fluid oz	600ml ($\frac{1}{2}$ litre)

$\frac{1}{4}$ pint	150ml	1$\frac{1}{2}$ pints	900ml
$\frac{1}{2}$ pint	300ml	1$\frac{3}{4}$ pints	1 litre
1 pint	570ml	2 pints	1150ml

Gas mark					
1	275°F	140°C	5	375°F	190°C
2	300°F	150°C	6	400°F	200°C
3	325°F	160°C	7	425°F	210°C
4	350°F	180°C	8	450°F	220°C

RECIPES FROM
NATIONAL TRUST
PROPERTIES

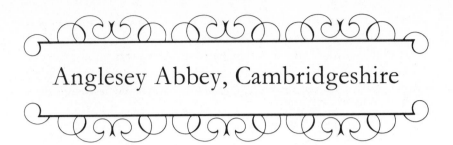

Anglesey Abbey, Cambridgeshire

Anglesey Abbey was originally an Augustinian priory inhabited by black-cowled canons who lived a structured austere life of prayer and meditation. Four centuries of secular ownership after the priory was dissolved in 1535 left only a shadowy ruin and it was this that Huttleston Broughton, 1st Lord Fairhaven, bought in 1926. He restored the structure, filled the house with fascinating treasures and created a wonderful garden round the Abbey.

Lord Fairhaven was a man out of his time. He had an 18th-century attitude to life. Funded by the fortune his father had made in American railroads, he was a passionate and dedicated patron and collector. Anglesey's rooms are on a domestic scale, but they are full of precious and beautiful paintings, furniture and *objets d'art*. Lord Fairhaven collected anything and everything in which he was interested and some of his enthusiasms are immediately apparent. There are 33 beautiful and unusual clocks, almost all of which are in working order, bird books and pictures in abundance, hundreds of paintings, drawings and prints of Windsor, bronzes, statuary, walking-sticks, snuff boxes, carvings and tapestries. Many great artists are represented on the walls, Canaletto and Claude Lorraine among them, and Thomas Gainsborough's paintbox is here. You will find elegant furniture by Chippendale and other pieces whose main interest lies in their former owners, such as a dressing-table that belonged to David Garrick the actor, Sir Robert Walpole's library table and a small chair which Shakespeare is reputed to have sat in.

I found Anglesey rather like a rich box of chocolates, mostly delicious, but with the odd item that was not to my taste. Lord Fairhaven's garden, on the other hand, is utterly charming. Created from the bleak Cambridgeshire fens only fifty years ago, it is a great garden on an 18th-century scale, combining formal avenues of glorious trees with the freer approach of the picturesque. Every turn reveals new delights, views and vistas, glimpses of water, bowers or beds of flowers. Stroll down the magnificent Emperors' Walk lined with busts and along the River Lode to the mill. On the first Sunday in the month you can see this in action and you can buy the flour from the shop. Anglesey's garden is rewarding at any time of year. There are spectacular wild flowers in spring, dahlias in late summer, and a magnificent herbaceous garden.

The Visitors' Centre at the entrance to the grounds contains the National Trust shop and a sunny, light and airy restaurant, where you can eat lunch and tea outside under a pergola on fine days. Bread and scones are baked with flour from Lode Mill. The scone recipe is given below. English cooking is a speciality – spiced bread pudding and jam roll are traditional country recipes, splendid for keeping the damp fen weather at bay on chilly days.

Beef and Mushroom Casserole in Red Wine

3lb (1.4kg) chuck steak, cubed

3 tablespoons seasoned flour

1 large sliced onion, or better still 8oz (225g) small whole onions

½ pint (300ml) beef stock

½ pint (300ml) red wine

1 teaspoon mixed herbs

8oz (225g) button mushrooms

Salt and pepper

Preheat oven: gas mark 3, 325°F, 160°C

Coat the cubed steak with seasoned flour and brown in a frying-pan with a little fat or oil – about 5 minutes. Transfer to a casserole. Add the sliced onion or small whole onions to the pan and fry for a few minutes. Sprinkle any remaining seasoned flour over the onions and stir in. Pour in the beef stock and bring to the boil; then add to the meat in the casserole with the red wine and mixed herbs. Cover the casserole and cook in the oven for approximately 1½ hours. Take out and add the button mushrooms and continue to cook for a further ½ hour or until the meat is tender. Check the seasoning before serving.

Baked Jam Roll

8oz (225g) self-raising flour

Pinch of salt

4oz (100g) shredded suet

About 7 tablespoons cold water

1lb (450g) pot of jam (strawberry, apricot, blackcurrant etc)

Preheat oven: gas mark 5, 375°F, 190°C

Grease a 1lb (450g) loaf tin. Sift the flour and salt in a bowl, then sprinkle in the suet and mix lightly with your hands to distribute evenly. Add enough cold water to give a light, elastic dough and knead gently until smooth and the mixture leaves the sides of the bowl clean. Roll out into an oblong about $\frac{1}{4}$in (6mm) thick. Spread evenly with jam and roll up. Trim the edges, use any pastry trimmings to decorate the top, and place in the greased loaf tin. Brush the top with beaten egg and bake in the oven for approximately 30 minutes until a pale golden brown. Serve hot with egg custard sauce (see below).

Egg Custard Sauce

$\frac{1}{2}$ pint (300ml) milk or single cream

3 egg yolks

1 level tablespoon caster sugar

1 level teaspoon cornflour

2 drops of vanilla essence

Heat the milk or cream in a saucepan to almost boiling. Blend the egg yolks, cornflour, sugar and vanilla essence together in a small bowl. Then pour in the hot milk or cream – stirring all the time – and return to the saucepan. Heat very gently (still stirring) until the sauce has thickened.

Serve hot with sweets or cool for a trifle. It will also freeze.

Honey Oat Cakes

2oz (50g) margarine

3 tablespoons clear honey

5oz (125g) light brown sugar

5oz (125g) coconut

2oz (50g) rolled oats

8oz (225g) wholemeal flour

1¼ teaspoons baking powder

Preheat oven: gas mark 3, 325°F, 160°C

Grease a baking tin approximately 10 × 7in (25 × 18cm). Melt the margarine and honey over a low heat. Mix all the dry ingredients together and add to the margarine and honey. Spread in the tin and bake in the oven for 20 minutes. Whilst still warm, cut into triangles and leave to cool in the tin.

Wholemeal Scones

8oz (225g) wholemeal flour

½oz (13g) baking powder

2oz (50g) lard

1oz (25g) soft brown sugar

1½oz (38g) sultanas (optional)

2fl oz (60ml) milk

1 egg

Preheat oven: gas mark 8, 450°F, 220°C

In a large mixing bowl sift the flour and the baking powder – add any bran left in the sieve. Rub in the diced fat with your fingertips until the mixture resembles coarse breadcrumbs. Add the sugar and optional fruit and combine evenly. Make a well in the centre and slowly add the egg and milk beaten together. Combine the flour by stirring it in with a fork to make a smooth dough. Knead slightly to make a ball and place on a floured board. Roll out to a thickness of not less than 1in (2.5cm) and cut out the scones using a 2in (5cm) cutter. Place on a greased baking tray and, if you like, brush with milk or dust with flour. Bake in a hot oven for 15 minutes.

Arlington Court, Devon

This elegant white, mainly Regency house is surrounded by grounds and gardens which mirror the affection which the property has always inspired in its owners – previously the Chichester family and now the Trust. Jacob sheep and small shaggy Shetland ponies graze in the park and by the lake and there are sunny sheltered seats against the wall of the kitchen garden.

Any visitor who has made a collection as a child or adult, and most of us have, will be fascinated by the contents of Arlington. Miss Rosalie Chichester, the last member of the family to live here, was a passionate collector. Here you can see wonderful displays of model ships and nautical pictures, a hundred pieces of pewter, snuff boxes and an extraordinary mixture of objects from all over the world. She was an inveterate traveller and liked to bring home souvenirs, as all tourists do. The difference was that she brought home thousands. Her shell collection alone filled 75 cabinets and visitors to the house today can see rare shells and encrusted boxes and dishes. Family memorabilia, a mysterious Blake painting, costumes, musical instruments, handsome furniture and above all a sense of the benign presence of this redoubtable, energetic Victorian lady make a visit to Arlington both fascinating and evocative of its era. Continuing the collecting tradition, the Trust has acquired over forty horse-drawn carriages which are on show in the stables, together with a display of harnesses.

Reviving lunches and teas are served in the old kitchen – a pretty

room decorated in brown and cream. Local recipes are used to produce hot nourishing casseroles, pies made with herb pastry, soups, and splendidly calorific puddings with seasonal ingredients like Exmoor In and Out and Blackcurrant Flummery. Local clotted cream is served with the puddings.

Leek Soup with Cream

1 large onion

1½lb (675g) leeks

2oz (50g) butter or margarine

2oz (50g) plain flour

1 tablespoon cream per serving and chopped parsley for garnish

1 stock cube (either chicken or vegetarian) made up to 1½ pints (900ml) of liquid with half milk and half water and a little chopped parsley

Salt and pepper to taste

Chop the onion and the leeks and sauté gently in the butter/margarine until soft but not coloured. Add the flour and stir well, then add the stock/milk and simmer until the vegetables are cooked. Taste and season with salt and pepper. This soup can either be liquidised at this point or served as it is. Either way it is nicest with a spoonful of cream added at the last minute and a scattering of chopped parsley.

Tomato, Orange and Mint Soup

1 medium onion

2oz (50g) butter or margarine

1½lb (675g) tomatoes (these need not be first quality, this is a good recipe to use up slightly squashy tomatoes; alternatively use the same weight of tinned tomatoes)

Rind and juice of one large orange

1 stock cube (chicken or vegetarian)

Worcester sauce, pepper and salt to taste

Chopped fresh mint to garnish

Peel, chop and sauté the onion gently in butter/margarine until soft but not coloured. Stir in the grated orange rind and pepper and salt and a spoonful of Worcester sauce. Then add the chopped tomatoes, stir well and simmer until cooked. Liquidise the mixture and dilute to required thickness with stock and orange juice. Adjust seasoning to taste, reheat and serve with a sprinkling of fresh mint on each bowl.

Herb Pastry

This is simply a favourite shortcrust pastry with the addition of either mixed herbs or one specific herb, depending on the contents of the pie. Use rosemary with a lamb pie, thyme with the chicken pie and mixed herbs with the pork squab pie.

Chicken Thyme Pie

4 chicken breasts (1 per person)

1 large onion

6 large sticks of celery

Fresh or dried thyme, salt and pepper to taste

2oz (50g) flour and ½ pint (300ml) milk

½ pint (300ml) chicken stock (make it with a stock cube if you have none fresh)

½ pint (300ml) of thick white sauce made with 2oz (50g) butter

To cover

Shortcrust pastry made with 10oz (275g) flour, 5oz (125g) butter/margarine and the addition of a heaped teaspoonful of thyme with the seasoning.

Preheat oven: gas mark 4, 350°F, 180°C

Slice and sauté the onion and slice the celery. Sauté the chicken breasts in a little butter/oil mixture until nice and brown. Lay in a pie dish with the onion and celery. Season with a little thyme, salt and pepper and cover with stock. Cover the dish with foil and cook gently in the oven until tender. Cool, make the thick white sauce and then stir it in to make a good thick mixture with the chicken. Cover the pie dish with the pastry, decorate with any oddments and glaze with milk. Put it back in the oven, increase the heat (gas mark 6, 400°F, 200°C) and cook for about 30 minutes until golden brown.

Pork Squab Pie

1lb (450g) diced lean fillet of pork
tossed in seasoned flour
(for quantities other than four,
allow 4oz (100g) per person)

Fresh or dried sage, salt and
pepper to taste

¾ pint (450ml) meat stock

1 large onion

3 Cox's apples, peeled and sliced

1lb (450g) cooked potatoes, diced
(if new they can be added whole
or halved)

A handful of raisins

To cover

Shortcrust pastry made with 10oz (275g) flour and 5oz (125g) butter/
margarine, with a dessertspoonful of mixed herbs added to the
seasoning.

Preheat oven: gas mark 4, 350°F, 180°C

Sauté the onion. Sauté the meat in a little butter/oil mixture until nice
and brown. Cut into chunks and lay in a pie dish with the onion. Season
with sage, pepper and salt and cover with the meat stock. Cover the dish
with foil and cook gently in the oven until tender (approx. 45 minutes).
Cool, then add the sliced apple, diced cooked potato and raisins. Cover
the pie dish with the pastry, decorate with any oddments, and glaze with
milk. Put it back in the oven, increase the heat (gas mark 6, 400°F,
200°C), and cook for about 30 minutes until golden brown.

Blackcurrant Flummery

1lb (450g) blackcurrants
½ pint (300ml) double cream
8oz (225g) caster sugar

1 egg white
Whipped cream to garnish

Make a thick sieved purée of the blackcurrants, stewed with a little
water. Allow to cool. Whip the cream with the caster sugar. Whip the
egg white separately and fold into the cream. Gently stir the cream
mixture into the purée so as to give a marbled effect and serve in
individual glasses garnished with a rosette of whipped cream. Chill
before serving. This is also excellent made with gooseberries.

Exmoor In and Out

2lb (900g) cooking apples (preferably Bramleys)

2oz (50g) demerara sugar mixed with 1 teaspoon cinnamon

4 tablespoons apple juice mixed with a few drops of almond essence

Topping

4oz (100g) butter

4oz (100g) demerara sugar

2 eggs

4oz (100g) self-raising flour

2oz (50g) ground almonds

A handful of flaked almonds

Preheat oven: gas mark 4, 350°F, 180°C

Peel and slice the apples into an ovenproof dish, drizzle the sugar, cinnamon and apple juice over the apples. Cover with a damp cloth while mixing the topping. Beat the butter and demerara sugar together until light and beat in the eggs gradually (this can be done in a food processor). Then fold in the flour and ground almonds. Spread on the apples and scatter over the handful of flaked almonds. Bake until golden brown – about 40 minutes.

A delicious recipe, but I have never been able to discover the reason for its name.

Attingham Park, Shropshire

Built very fast by the 1st Lord Berwick in the late 18th century to announce to all who saw it that the newly-created peer had arrived in society, Attingham Park is a striking example of conspicuous expenditure.

Astonishingly, the splendid symmetrical Classical building actually encloses an older, smaller house within itself. The state rooms were designed to be as grand as possible – the entrance hall has huge pillars, the picture gallery is immense, the drawing-room has elegant Empire furniture and an Adam-style ceiling. But pride comes before a fall. The 2nd Lord Berwick spent lavishly on altering and decorating the house and on collecting paintings and furniture. In 1827 the money ran out, Lord Berwick retired sadly abroad and virtually the entire contents were sold. Happily the 3rd Lord Berwick, who had been Ambassador in Italy, refurnished the house splendidly. Down in the vaults there is a marvellous collection of Regency silver which he amassed.

Attingham then suffered from considerable neglect until 1919, when Teresa Hulton married Thomas Henry, the 8th Lord Berwick. She loved the house, restored the state rooms and lived in it until her death in 1972. Her favourite room was the Boudoir, delicately painted in late 18th-century French fashion. The lemon madeira cake was also her favourite; perhaps a little plain for today's taste, it is best sampled with a glass of Madeira!

In the hall you can see Humphry Repton's 'Red Book' for Attingham, in which the great landscape gardener set out his projected designs. The

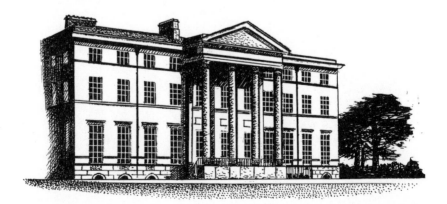

park is now being replanted to his original plans and it is a delightful place for a stroll. There is an 18th-century bee house and an ice-house and a herd of fallow deer under the trees.

The handsome Steward's Room is now the tea-room and is hung with paintings of prize horses and cows. Lunches on Sundays and home-made teas are served on Spode Italian china exactly as might have been used in the Attingham Servants' Hall. On colder days there is a comforting log fire and if it is fine and warm tea can be taken outside in the lovely surroundings of Attingham park. The Shrewsbury biscuits, made to a very old local recipe, are a feature of the teas.

Cheesy Leek and Cauliflower Flan

8oz (225g) shortcrust pastry

½ cauliflower

2 leeks

2oz (50g) butter

1oz (25g) plain flour

½ pint (300ml) milk

4oz (100g) strong Cheddar cheese, grated

Salt and pepper

Preheat oven: gas mark 5, 375°F, 190°C

Grease and line an 8in (20cm) flan dish with rolled out pastry. Bake 'blind' for 15 minutes in the oven. Cook the cauliflower until tender, break into florets and spread over the flan case. Cut the leeks into rings about ¾in (2cm) wide and wash well. Melt ½oz (13g) butter in a small saucepan, add the leeks, cover and cook for a few minutes. Meanwhile, melt the remaining butter, stir in the flour over a low heat until completely absorbed, pour in the milk and cook, stirring all the time until the sauce is smooth and thick. Stir in the grated cheese and as soon as it has melted add the leeks and season to taste. Pour the mixture over the cauliflower in the flan case and serve at once. This also tastes good cold.

Apple Cake

6oz (175g) self-raising flour
1 teaspoon mixed spice – optional
8oz (225g) sugar
8oz (225g) butter

6 cooking apples
2 eggs beaten
Milk to mix

Preheat oven: gas mark 5, 375°F, 190°C

Grease a 9 × 9in (23 × 23cm) tin. Sift the flour and mixed spice together and put into a bowl with the sugar. Roughly chop in the butter but do not rub in or cream. Peel the apples and slice into the mixture. Add the beaten eggs and enough milk to make a fairly stiff batter. Bake in the tin for about 1½ hours – until golden brown.

This can also be made with pears or plums. It is delicious served hot with thin cream; any left over can be eaten as cake.

Lemon Madeira Cake

4oz (100g) soft butter
5oz (125g) caster sugar
2 eggs

Rind and juice of 1 lemon
8oz (225g) self-raising flour

Preheat oven: gas mark 2, 300°F, 150°C

Grease and line a 6in (15cm) round deep cake tin. Cream together the butter and sugar until light and fluffy. Beat in the eggs a little at a time; then add the rind and juice of a lemon. Gently fold in the flour using a large metal spoon and spoon the mixture into the lined cake tin. Place in the centre of the oven and bake for approximately 1 hour.

This is particularly good with a glass of Madeira.

Tea Loaf

12fl oz (360ml) cold tea

7oz (200g) soft brown sugar

3oz (75g) sultanas

3oz (75g) currants

3oz (75g) raisins

3oz (75g) mixed peel

10oz (275g) self-raising flour

1 egg, beaten

The night before, put the cold tea, sugar and dried fruit in a bowl; cover and leave to soak overnight.

Preheat oven: gas mark 4, 350°F, 180°C

Grease and base line either a 2lb (900g) loaf tin or an 8in (20cm) round cake tin. Mix the soaked fruit and sugar plus the liquid into the flour. Add the beaten egg to make a smooth mixture. Turn into the greased tin and bake in a moderate oven for about 1 hour 45 minutes. When cooked, cool on a wire tray.

Serve sliced with butter.

Shrewsbury Biscuits

2oz (50g) butter

2oz (50g) sugar

1 egg

2oz (50g) currants

6oz (175g) plain flour

$\frac{1}{2}$ teaspoon mixed spice

Caster sugar to decorate

Preheat oven: gas mark 5, 375°F, 190°C

Grease two large baking sheets. Cream the butter and sugar until pale and fluffy. Add the egg and beat in well. Fold in the currants, flour and mixed spice and knead lightly into a smooth ball. Roll out on a floured surface to about $\frac{1}{4}$in (5mm) thickness. Cut into rounds with a $2\frac{1}{2}$in (6cm) fluted cutter and put on the baking trays. Bake in the oven for 15 minutes – after 5 minutes take out and sprinkle with caster sugar; then continue to cook until firm and very light brown in colour. Makes approximately 20 biscuits.

This is a very old recipe. Shrewsbury biscuits are mentioned in a document of 1561 but were probably made well before this date.

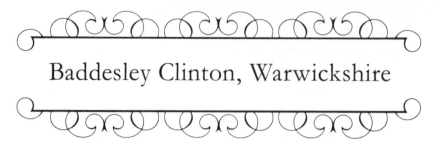

Baddesley Clinton, Warwickshire

Baddesley Clinton is a small moated manor in the Forest of Arden. In medieval times this was not a forest in the modern sense of the word and would have more closely resembled rough pasture dotted with clumps of trees. Perhaps this is what Shakespeare had in mind when he set his *As You Like It* here! Today the house lies in green fields and parkland full of contented cows.

The Ferrers family lived at Baddesley Clinton from 1517 until it came to the Trust in 1980 and held on to the property through thick and thin. As staunch Catholics, they made their house a sanctuary for fellow believers and the Mass was said in secret here. Paradoxically, the family's religious sympathies were in some ways an advantage for they helped to ensure that Baddesley Clinton escaped change. It is a delightful survival, externally much as it was in the 1580s when Henry Ferrers, known as 'the Antiquary', built the great hall and filled the house with panelling and armorial glass in glowing colours.

Cross the moat, walk through the sturdy gateway and you are in a

sunny courtyard, planted out in the colours of the Ferrers' shield. Inside the house, there are rooms, pictures and possessions which vividly evoke Baddesley Clinton's turbulent history. Ten men evaded discovery in 1591 by sheltering in a garderobe in the corner of the old kitchen and there are other hiding-places in the moat room and the front bedroom. The bloodstain in front of the fireplace in the solar is said to have resulted from a murder long ago. There is good furniture and interesting china everywhere. Many of the pictures are 19th-century, painted by Rebecca Dulcibella Orpen, wife of Marmion Ferrers. It was largely due to her memorable aunt, the 19th-century novelist Lady Chatterton, who also lived at Baddesley Clinton, that the fortunes of the house revived in the last century. She it was, for example, who built the little chapel.

Beyond the house are stewponds full of fat roach and meadows kept deliberately wild for conservation – the atmosphere of rural tranquillity is very soothing.

The estate has always been a working farm and it is particularly appropriate that you buy tickets and shop in the cowshed and eat lunches and teas in the barn, built by Thomas Ferrers in 1721. The buildings are simple but mellow and on a sunny day it is a pleasure to sample the good home-made soups, quiches and salads, puddings and cakes at a table in the stable-yard.

Spinach Quiche with Wholemeal Pastry

8oz (225g) wholemeal pastry
(made with hard margarine)

8oz (225g) spinach, cooked and
well chopped

4oz (100g) sieved cottage cheese

2 large eggs

5fl oz (150ml) milk

Grated nutmeg

Salt and pepper

Preheat oven: gas mark 7, 425°F, 210°C

Grease and line an 8in (20cm) flan tin with wholemeal pastry. Prick the bottom with a fork and brush with egg white. Cook for 15 minutes and then turn down the oven temperature to gas mark 4, 350°F, 180°C. Place the cooked spinach and sieved cottage cheese into the pastry case. Whisk the eggs and milk with the seasoning and pour over the mixture. Bake in a moderate oven for approximately $\frac{3}{4}$ hour, or until the custard is set and light brown. Sliced tomatoes can be put on top for decoration.

Perfect served hot, warm or cold.

Gingerbread Pudding

4oz (100g) butter

8oz (225g) golden syrup

3oz (75g) granulated sugar

1 tablespoon orange marmalade

1 large egg

$\frac{1}{4}$ pint (150ml) milk

8oz (225g) self-raising flour

1 teaspoon ground ginger

1 teaspoon bicarbonate of soda

1 teaspoon cinnamon

Preheat oven: gas mark 2, 300°F, 150°C

Grease an 8in (20cm) square tin. Put the butter, sugar, golden syrup and marmalade into a saucepan and heat until the sugar has dissolved. Leave to cool. Beat the egg with the milk and add to the syrup mixture. Sift the flour with the ginger, cinnamon and bicarbonate of soda, pour into the mixture and beat until smooth. Turn into the prepared tin and bake in the oven for $\frac{1}{2}$–$\frac{3}{4}$ hour, or until firm.

Serve hot with cream. Fattening, but very comforting on a cold day.

Luscious Cake

3oz (75g) raisins

2 tablespoons brandy

5oz (125g) soft margarine

5oz (125g) caster sugar

2 eggs

1lb (450g) mincemeat

7oz (200g) self-raising flour

1oz (25g) cocoa

Topping
4oz (100g) glacé cherries

2oz (50g) walnut pieces

4oz (100g) apricot jam

Preheat oven: gas mark 3, 325°F, 160°C

Grease and line an 8in (20cm) cake tin. Soak the raisins in the brandy for 10 minutes. Cream together the margarine and caster sugar until light and fluffy. Beat in the eggs one at a time and then mix in the mincemeat and the raisins in brandy. Sieve together the flour and cocoa and gently fold into the mixture. Turn into the lined tin and cook for approximately 2 hours.

Topping
Halve the glacé cherries and put into a saucepan with the nuts and jam.

Stir continuously until boiling; spread immediately onto the cake as soon as it comes out of the oven.

This cake will freeze well. What a good name for this rich, fruity mixture

Wholemeal Cheese Scones

1lb (450g) wholemeal flour

2 teaspoons baking powder

1 tablespoon mixed herbs (own choice, preferably freshly chopped)

5oz (125g) margarine or half margarine/half lard

4oz (100g) grated cheese (sharp flavour – mature Cheddar or Stilton are both very tasty)

$\frac{1}{2}$ pint (300ml) milk

Preheat oven: gas mark 7, 425°F, 210°C

Grease a large baking sheet. Mix together the flour, baking powder and herbs. Rub in the margarine until the mixture resembles breadcrumbs. Add most of the grated cheese, leaving about 1 tablespoon. Using a knife, gradually mix in the milk until you have a soft dough. Knead lightly with your hands. Next roll out the dough to $\frac{3}{4}$in (2cm) thick and cut out the scones using a $2\frac{1}{4}$in (6cm) cutter. Place the scones on the baking sheet, brush with a little milk, then sprinkle the remaining grated cheese over the top. Bake in a hot oven for about 15–20 minutes.

Makes around 12 scones. Warm and buttered, these are very good with soup instead of rolls.

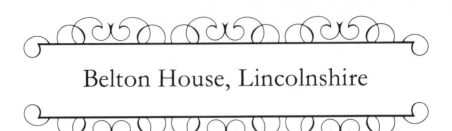

Belton House, Lincolnshire

Belton House is a great landowner's residence set as such residences should be in rolling parkland stocked with fat sheep and somnolent cows grazing beneath horse chestnuts and limes.

Twelve generations of the Brownlow and Cust families owned Belton until 1983 when the house was given to the Trust. Belton as we know it was built in 1684–88 by Sir John Brownlow. There is an extraordinary picture of the house at that period on the west staircase in which 'Henry Bugg', Sir John's porter, figures prominently in the centre – more understandable when you learn he was the painter. The rooms are spacious, with elegant furniture and pictures. Family portraits by Reynolds and Romney and other old masters, and vast calm garden scenes by Melchior d'Hondecoeter line the walls. The wood carvings are intricate, fascinating and very beautiful – those in the Saloon may be by Grinling Gibbons himself. I was also struck by the richly-glowing oriental bowls and plates in what is now called the Ante Library, and by the unusual painted floor in the Tyrconnel Room. The Chapel Drawing-Room next door has 'two pieces of Dutch Hangeings' set into the panelling, with exotic delicate designs based on Indian Moghul miniatures.

On a lighter note, the exercise chair in the library should not be missed. It was made in 1754 for Viscount Tyrconnel, who sought a substitute for riding in arthritic old age. The most poignant association at Belton is more recent. The late Lord Brownlow was a great friend and confidant of Edward VIII. As Prince of Wales, he often stayed at Belton, sleeping in the delightful Chinese Bedroom. Peaceful Belton must have been a good refuge for the troubled prince.

Lunch and tea at Belton are served in the stable restaurant, sunny, light and airy with a brick floor and cream walls. Delicious quiches and tarts are a speciality. Grantham gingerbreads are a local recipe, a crisp appetising alternative to parkin and other gingerbreads.

Vegetarian Quiche with Wholemeal Pastry

12oz (350g) wholemeal pastry
(made with hard margarine)

1lb (450g) any mixed vegetables,
cooked or uncooked

4oz (100g) sliced mushrooms

3 eggs, lightly beaten

½ pint (300ml) milk

Salt and pepper to taste

Preheat oven: gas mark 4, 350°F, 180°C

Grease and line a 10in (25cm) flan dish with wholemeal pastry. Place the cooked vegetables, mushrooms and seasoning into the uncooked case. Mix the beaten eggs with the milk and pour into the case. Bake in the oven for approximately 45 minutes or until set.

Smoked Mackerel Quiche

12 oz (350g) shortcrust pastry

3 medium smoked mackerel
fillets, flaked

Sprinkling of mixed herbs

Pepper

3 eggs, lightly beaten

½ pint (300ml) milk

Preheat oven: gas mark 4, 350°F, 180°C

Line a greased 10in (25cm) flan case with the shortcrust pastry. Place the flaked fish evenly in the uncooked pastry case and add the seasoning. Mix the beaten eggs with the milk and pour into the case. Bake in the oven for approximately 45 minutes or until set.

Coconut Bakewell Tart

12oz (350g) shortcrust pastry
2oz (50g) margarine
2oz (50g) sugar
1 large egg, beaten

1oz (25g) desiccated coconut
2oz (50g) ground rice
3–4 tablespoons jam or lemon curd

Icing

4–6oz (100–175g) sifted icing sugar
2–4 drops vanilla essence
1–2 tablespoons warm water

Preheat oven: gas mark 4, 350°F, 180°C

Grease a 10in (25cm) flan dish and line with the shortcrust pastry. Cream together the margarine and sugar until light and fluffy and gradually add the beaten egg. Mix in the desiccated coconut and ground rice. Spread the uncooked pastry case with jam or lemon curd, spoon in the mixture and spread evenly. If you have any pastry left over, make some lattice strips for the top. Bake in the oven for about 1 hour or until firm. Allow to cool, then cover with icing.

Icing

Put the sifted icing sugar and (if you wish) a few drops of vanilla essence in a basin and gradually add the warm water. The icing should be thick enough to coat the back of a spoon. If necessary, add more water or sugar to adjust the consistency.

Bakewell Tart used to be called Bakewell Pudding. Tradition has it that it was first made in the Rutland Arms at Bakewell by a cook who misunderstood the instructions she had been given for a strawberry tart!

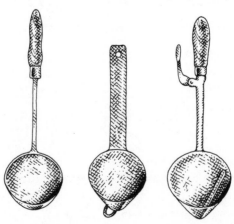

Home-made Ice-cream

1 pint (570ml) double cream

4 tablespoons milk

2 teaspoons vanilla essence

10 level tablespoons sifted icing sugar

Beat the cream and milk together in a bowl until the mixture has thickened slightly. Add the vanilla essence and icing sugar and mix gently until well combined. Pour into a tray or carton and place in the freezer for approximately 1 hour or until the edges of the mixture have frozen. Empty back into the bowl and mix lightly – return to the freezer and freeze until firm.

Treacle Tart

12oz (350g) shortcrust pastry

10oz (275g) golden syrup

1oz (25g) margarine

2oz (50g) oats

Preheat oven: gas mark 4, 350°F, 180°C

Grease a 10in (25cm) flan dish and line with the shortcrust pastry. Melt the syrup and margarine gently together in a saucepan, add the oats and pour into the uncooked pastry case. If you have any pastry left over, roll out and cut into strips to make a lattice on top. Bake in the oven for approximately 35 minutes or until set.

Coconut Crunch

4oz (100g) margarine

2oz (50g) sugar

1 cup desiccated coconut

6 teaspoons chocolate powder

1 cup self-raising flour

Icing

6oz (175g) icing sugar

2 level teaspoons cocoa

$2\frac{1}{2}$ tablespoons hot water

Preheat oven: gas mark 3, 325°F, 160°C

Grease a small Swiss roll tin. Cream together the margarine and sugar. Add the coconut, chocolate powder and self-raising flour. Place in the greased tin and cook for 45 minutes or until firm and dry.

Icing

Sift the icing sugar into a basin. Dissolve the cocoa in the hot water and gradually add to the icing sugar. The icing should be thick enough to coat the back of a spoon. If necessary, add more water or sugar to adjust the consistency. Spread the coconut crunch with the chocolate topping while the mixture is warm (not hot) and cut into pieces when cold.

Grantham Gingerbreads

4oz (100g) margarine	2–3 teaspoons ground ginger
12oz (350g) sugar	9oz (250g) self-raising flour
1 egg, beaten	

Preheat oven: gas mark 1½, 280°F, 145°C

Grease a large baking tray. Beat the margarine in a bowl with a wooden spoon to soften it, then work in the sugar followed by the beaten egg. Sift the ground ginger into the flour and add to the mixture, which will be quite dry and crumbly – a bit like shortbread. Using your hands, bring the mixture together into about thirty small balls the size of a walnut and place on the baking tray, leaving plenty of space between each one. Cook in the oven for 30 minutes. The gingerbreads should remain pale in colour and have a texture and appearance rather like a macaroon.

A crispy alternative to the more traditional parkin.

Grantham Gingerbreads were first made in 1740 when a local baker muddled the ingredients for another type of biscuit. Grantham is now known as the Gingerbread town and the local football team are called the Gingerbreads!

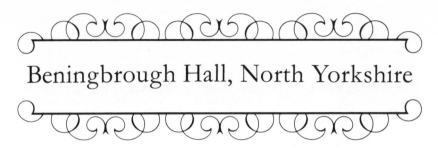

Beningbrough Hall, North Yorkshire

Beningbrough is a very grand house indeed. Magnificently Baroque, and flanked by two small pavilions topped by cupolas, it looms over the misty water-meadows of the Vale of York. It is a highly contrived house, where the eye is constantly being drawn to new views and vistas both inside and out. But although grand, it is neither forbidding nor overwhelming, partly because it is built in a peculiarly mellow small red brick.

Outside, wander in the American garden or in the two formal gardens laid out by Lady Chesterfield, who loved the house and was the wife of the last owner. Walk away from the building and look back; Beningbrough was designed to give pleasure from every angle. Built in the early years of the 18th century by John Bourchier, the architect/builder was a local man, William Thornton. It seems likely that the exterior plans were heavily influenced by the famous Baroque architect, Thomas Archer, but Thornton himself takes credit for the rich decorative interiors.

Beningbrough is sparsely furnished in the original mode so that the eye can appreciate the views through the house as Mr Thornton undoubtedly intended. Much of the furniture, like the house itself, is both beautiful and grand. The subtle greens and greys on the walls have been specially and meticulously mixed to match the original colours found under layers of later paint. The wonderful wood carving in the drawing-room would originally have been painted, which is why no

attempt was made to conceal the joins or to match the colours of the different woods. Each state bedchamber has its dressing-room and closet. The closets have delightful corner overmantels now crowded with arrangements of fine late 17th- and early 18th-century Chinese porcelain. Handsome portraits of 18th-century notables lent by the National Portrait Gallery are hung throughout the house and the Gallery has mounted a fascinating exhibition on the second floor entitled 'History of Portraits'.

Do not miss the Victorian laundry, refitted with mangles, presses, flat-irons and other equipment, and with racks hung with lovely white lacy Victorian undergarments.

The restaurant at Beningbrough is in a south-facing courtyard bright with flowers and is cheerful, sunny and warm. Here you can eat delicious hot or cold lunches. There is always a dish for vegetarians and puddings include modern versions of old favourites such as summer pudding. At tea-time, you can enjoy home-made cakes and scones which continue the English tradition, and are freshly baked in the restaurant kitchens.

Lady Chesterfield's Tomato Soup

2oz (50g) butter	1 small bouquet garni
2 rashers streaky bacon	$\frac{1}{2}$ dessertspoon sugar
1 medium onion	1oz (25g) plain flour
1 carrot, peeled and diced	$\frac{1}{2}$ pint (300ml) milk
1 stick celery	Salt and pepper
1lb (450g) tomatoes, roughly chopped	Single cream and deep fried croutons to serve
1$\frac{1}{2}$ pints (900ml) stock	

Melt 1oz (25g) of the butter and sweat the diced bacon and the onion until the onion is soft but not coloured. Then add the carrot, celery and tomatoes, the stock, bouquet garni and sugar. Bring the mixture to the boil and simmer for approximately 1 hour. Take out the bouquet garni and liquidise the mixture. Blend the remaining 1oz butter with the flour and $\frac{1}{2}$ pint of milk and whisk this into the vegetable purée. You will need to whisk it to stop lumps forming. Reheat the soup, season to taste with salt and pepper and serve very hot with a swirl of cream in each bowl and fried croutons.

Cauliflower, Onion and Mushroom Special

1 large cauliflower divided into florets

Butter for frying

1 medium sized onion, peeled and finely chopped

6oz (175g) button mushrooms, sliced

1oz (25g) grated cheese

Cheese Sauce

1½oz (38g) butter

3 level tablespoons flour

½ pint (300ml) milk

3oz (75g) grated cheese

Cayenne pepper

Cook the cauliflower in boiling salted water for 10 minutes or until tender and place in an ovenproof dish. Now make the cheese sauce. Melt the butter in a saucepan, stir in the flour and cook for 2–3 minutes. Remove the pan from the heat and gradually stir in the milk; bring to the boil and continue to stir until it thickens. Add the 3oz (75g) grated cheese and season to taste. In a small saucepan fry the onions and sliced mushrooms for two or three minutes and add to the cheese sauce. Pour over the cauliflower, sprinkle with the rest of the grated cheese and place under a hot grill for a few minutes until nice and golden. Serve immediately.

Beef Layer Pie with Yoghurt Topping

1 medium onion, chopped

1oz (25g) butter

8oz (225g) cooked roast beef, minced

¼ teaspoon dried mixed herbs

2 level tablespoons tomato purée

1 teaspoon Worcester sauce

Salt and pepper

1lb (450g) potatoes

8oz (225g) tomatoes, skinned and sliced

1 egg, beaten

1oz (25g) flour

5oz (125g) natural yoghurt

Paprika

Preheat oven: gas mark 5, 375°F, 190°C

In a saucepan cook the onion gently in the butter. Add the minced meat, mixed herbs, tomato purée and Worcester sauce and season to taste. Meanwhile boil the potatoes until tender but not soft, and slice them. In a 2 pint (1200ml) ovenproof casserole, arrange a layer of potato slices, followed by a layer of the meat mixture, then the tomatoes, finishing with a layer of potatoes. Cover and bake in the oven for 30 minutes.

Blend the flour and yoghurt with the beaten egg. Season to taste and spoon over the pie after it has cooked for 30 minutes. Return the dish to the oven and cook for a further 30 minutes. Dust with paprika before serving.

This recipe is an excellent way to use up the remains of your Sunday roast.

Muesli Crumble

1½lb (700g) fruit of your choice,
e.g. apples, plums, gooseberries, rhubarb

4–6oz (100–175g) sugar

Crumble Topping

2oz (50g) butter

4oz (100g) wholemeal flour

4oz (100g) brown sugar

3oz (75g) muesli

Preheat oven: gas mark 4, 350°F, 180°C

Prepare the fruit and layer with the sugar in an ovenproof dish. Rub the butter into the flour until the mixture is the texture of fine crumbs, then stir in the sugar and muesli. Sprinkle the mixture on top of the prepared fruit and bake in the oven for about 45 minutes to 1 hour, or until the fruit is cooked and the crumble golden brown.

Serve with custard or cream.

Summer Pudding

1¼lb (700g) mixed soft fruit
(blackcurrants, redcurrants, raspberries)
5oz (125g) caster sugar
7–8 medium slices of white bread

Lightly butter a 1½ pint (900ml) pudding basin. Prepare and wash the fruit and place in a saucepan with the sugar. Cook gently for 3–5 minutes until the juices run and the sugar has melted. Line the base and sides of the pudding basin with the bread, making sure that there are no gaps between the slices. Reserve two slices for the top. Pour the fruit in (except for a cupful of juice) and cover the top with the reserved bread slices. Put a small plate or saucer over the pudding (one that fits inside the rim of the bowl), place a weight on top and chill overnight. Unmould by holding a serving platter over the top and turning the pudding over. Use the reserved juice to spoon over and soak any bits of bread that still look white. Serve cut into slices with some thick cream.

Best made in season, but try it with frozen fruit for a taste of summer in the winter.

Date and Walnut Scones

2oz (50g) butter

8oz (225g) wholemeal self-raising flour

1 tablespoon light soft brown sugar

3oz (75g) chopped dates

1oz (25g) chopped walnuts

5 tablespoons milk

Preheat oven: gas mark 8, 450°F, 220°C

Lightly grease a baking sheet. Rub the fat into the flour until the mixture resembles fine breadcrumbs. Stir in the sugar, dates and walnuts, then mix with milk to a pliable, not sticky dough. Knead gently on a lightly floured surface until smooth and free from cracks. Roll out to 1½in (4cm) thick, cut out the scones using a 2in (5cm) cutter, and place on the greased baking sheet. Brush the tops with milk and bake in the oven for 10 minutes. Cool on a wire rack.

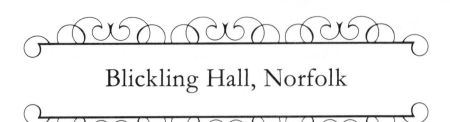

Blickling Hall, Norfolk

Built of rose-red brick, gabled and turreted, Blickling will satisfy everybody's idea of what a country house should be. The visitor approaches this lovely Jacobean building down a wide forecourt lined with vast ancient yew hedges, 10 feet wide and 17 feet high and immaculately clipped. The delightful grassy moat is beautifully planted with fuchsias, camellias, hydrangeas and old roses.

The entrance hall is as imposing and splendid as any in England, dominated by a huge staircase with spreading double flights and tall newel posts crowned with carved wooden figures. The wood gleams in the light from the massive stained-glass window halfway up. Interesting paintings and pieces of furniture abound, but Blickling is particularly

famous for its plaster ceilings. Edward Stanyon's Jacobean panels showing 'emblems and devices' in the Long Gallery are intriguing, blending extraordinarily well with the Victorian Arts and Crafts decoration. The gallery also contains a great library of rare books. The delicate Chinese Bedroom, with its 18th-century furniture and hand-painted wallpaper, is a total contrast. There is also a splendid tapestry of Peter the Great of Russia in a room specially designed to house it.

The Reptons, Humphry and his son John Adey, were much involved in landscaping the garden. The grounds include a lake with reeds and waterfowl and a formal woodland garden with an elegant Doric temple reached from the lovely parterre. An 18th-century orangery and a secret garden with a little summer-house are other pleasures.

Satisfy the inner man in the stable restaurant. Norfolk has been called the 'vegetable basket of England' and pride of place goes to dishes using local produce. Christmas lunches are popular at Blickling. Do try the Norfolk gingerbread, a local speciality, and also the fresh and fruity local apple wine.

Almond Cake

8oz (225g) soft margarine	8oz (225g) plain flour
8oz (225g) caster sugar	1 teaspoon baking powder
4 eggs	2oz (50g) ground almonds
1 teaspoon almond essence	1oz (25g) flaked almonds

Preheat oven: gas mark 3, 325°F, 160°C

Grease and line a 9in (23cm) cake tin. Cream together the margarine and sugar until pale and fluffy. Beat in the eggs one at a time. Add the almond essence. Sift together the flour and the baking powder and lightly fold into the cake mixture. Finally stir in the ground almonds. Spoon into the prepared cake tin and sprinkle the flaked almonds on top. Bake in the oven for approximately 1½ hours.

Blickling All-in-one Fruit Cake

8oz (225g) self-raising flour	2oz (50g) peel
4oz (100g) soft margarine	1½oz (38g) cherries
4oz (100g) caster sugar	2 eggs
2oz (50g) sultanas	4 tablespoons milk
2oz (50g) currants	

Preheat oven. gas mark 3, 325°F, 160°C

Grease and line a 9in (23cm) cake tin. This is an 'all-in-one' cake. Place all the ingredients into a large bowl and mix together until well combined – really soft margarine is needed for this. Spoon the mixture into the prepared cake tin and level it out. Bake in a moderate oven for 1–1½ hours, or until the centre is firm to touch. Let the cake cool in the tin before taking it out.

A marvellous last-minute recipe which takes only a few minutes to put together.

Caraway Cake

6oz (175g) soft margarine	1 pinch salt
6oz (175g) caster sugar	1 teaspoon baking powder
3 eggs	1 tablespoon ground almonds
3 teaspoons caraway seeds	1 tablespoon milk
8oz (225g) plain flour	

Preheat oven: gas mark 3, 325°F, 160°C

Grease and line a 9in (23cm) cake tin. Cream together the margarine and sugar until fluffy and pale. Add the eggs one at a time, beating well after each addition; then mix in the caraway seeds. Sift the flour, salt and baking powder together and fold gently into the mixture. Then add the ground almonds and milk. Spoon into the prepared tin, level out, and bake for approximately 1 hour or until firm to touch.

This is in the English tradition of good plain cakes – perfect at coffee time when you want something that is not too rich.

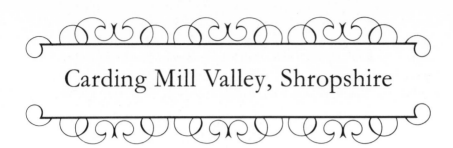

Carding Mill Valley, Shropshire

Put on your walking shoes to visit Carding Mill Valley. This beautiful spot with its interesting relics of the Industrial Revolution is part of the Long Mynd in the Shropshire hills, a moorland plateau (from which there are wonderful views) furrowed by green valleys.

There are excellent walks to suit both the serious walker and the less energetic or able, some on ancient paths and trackways. Animals, birds and plants abound. This is the most southerly grouse moor in Europe, and you may see red grouse on the hills, and buzzards or ravens gliding overhead. The stream banks are decorated with the delicate pink flowers of the bog pimpernel and the sinister insect-eating sundew and butterwort. Brown trout and bullhead fish can be glimpsed in the water and dippers dart from side to side.

Carding Mill itself is a steep-sided green valley. The rushing stream tumbling from the Lightspout Waterfall at its head was first used in medieval times to turn the wheel of a corn mill. Between 1800 and 1871 the mill was used for carding, spinning and weaving wool, but it was always a small enterprise and had difficulty competing with the huge mechanised mills in the north. By 1881 ginger beer and soda-water were being made in part of the premises and another part was a tea-room 'for the accommodation of visitors to the hills, the Carding Mill Valley being a favourite resort of excursionists'. So it is in the 1980s. The Chalet Pavilion, today's tea-room and café, was built in 1920. Stout shoes, rucksacks and hungry mouths are welcome here and walkers will find

hearty healthy food to eat on the spot or take into the hills. At the end of the day, hot tea and coffee and generous slices of home-made cake will satisfy appetites sharpened by the clear country air on this most beautiful piece of moorland.

Cheese and Onion Slice

Wholemeal flaky pastry
8oz (225g) self-raising wholemeal flour
6oz (175g) margarine, or half margarine/half lard
¼ pint (150ml) ice-cold water
Squeeze of lemon juice
Pinch of salt

Filling
1lb (450g) onions, finely chopped
6oz–8oz (175–225g) grated cheese

Preheat oven: gas mark 4, 350°F, 180°C

Pastry

Rub in half the fat with the flour until the mixture resembles fine breadcrumbs. Mix in the water and lemon juice a little at a time until a stiff consistency is achieved. Roll out on a floured surface and dot with a third of the remaining margarine. Fold and roll again, dotting the pastry with half the remaining fat – continue this way until all the fat is incorporated.

Filling

Roll out the pastry and line a 9in (23cm) flan tin or dish which has been well greased. Fry the onions gently until clear, place in the flan case and cover with the grated cheese. With the pastry leftovers, cut some strips and make a lattice on top of the flan – glaze with beaten egg and cook in the oven until the cheese is bubbling and the pastry cooked (approximately 40 minutes). Serve hot.

Mushroom and Onion Pasties

Wholemeal flaky pastry
Use the recipe for Cheese and Onion Slice above,
but double the quantity.

Filling

1 tablespoon oil

1lb (450g) onions, finely chopped

1 clove garlic, crushed

8oz (225g) mushrooms, wiped
and sliced

¼ teaspoon cayenne pepper

2 teaspoons fresh or dried mixed
herbs

2 hard-boiled eggs

Salt and pepper

Beaten egg for glazing

Preheat oven: gas mark 7, 425°F, 210°C

Make the pastry and refrigerate while you make the filling. Heat the oil
and gently fry the onion and garlic for 3–4 minutes. Add the mushrooms, herbs and cayenne pepper and cook over a gentle heat in a
covered pan for 10 minutes. Remove from the heat. Chop the hard-
boiled eggs coarsely and add to the mixture – season to taste and allow to
cool completely.

Roll out the pastry and cut into circles with a large saucer. Brush the
edges with beaten egg, then spoon 1–2 tablespoons of the filling on to
each round and seal. Brush the outside with egg glaze and make a small
hole in the centre. Place in the fridge for 30 minutes before baking to rest
the pastry. Bake in the oven for 15–20 minutes.

Makes 1 dozen.

Apple Cake

8oz (225g) plain flour

½ teaspoon ground cinnamon

½ teaspoon mixed spice

½ teaspoon bicarbonate of soda

4oz (100g) butter

6oz (175g) light soft brown sugar

2 eggs

4oz (100g) currants

6oz (175g) sultanas

2oz (50g) chopped walnuts

8oz (225g) cooking apples, peeled
and coarsely grated

Grated rind of a lemon

Preheat oven: gas mark 4, 350°F, 180°C

Grease and line an 8in (20cm) cake tin. Sift the flour, spices and soda together. In a separate bowl cream the butter and sugar until light and fluffy and pale in colour. Beat in the eggs one at a time, following each with a spoonful of the flour mixture. Fold in the remaining flour followed by the currants, sultanas and walnuts. Finally add the grated apple and lemon rind. Turn into the tin, level the top and bake in the oven for $1\frac{1}{4}$–$1\frac{1}{2}$ hours, or until the cake is firm to the touch and a skewer inserted in the centre comes out clean. Turn out and cool on a wire rack.

This is an excellent picnic cake, which keeps very well wrapped in cling film or foil.

Cinnamon Sticky Cake

4 eggs, separated

5oz (125g) caster sugar

4oz (100g) unsalted butter (very soft)

8oz (225g) plain flour

2 teaspoons baking powder

1 tablespoon ground cinnamon

2 tablespoons brandy (optional)

4oz (100g) raisins

4fl oz (120ml) milk

For the topping

3 tablespoons golden granulated sugar

$\frac{1}{2}$ teaspoon cinnamon

$\frac{1}{2}$oz (13g) butter

Preheat oven: gas mark 4, 350°F, 180°C

Grease and line a 9in (23cm) square cake tin. Beat the egg yolks with the sugar until very thick and pale and the whisk leaves a ribbon trail when lifted. Cream the butter until very soft and then beat into the egg mixture. Sift the flour with the baking powder and cinnamon and carefully fold into the mixture with the brandy, raisins and milk. When evenly mixed, fold in the stiffly whisked egg whites and spoon into the prepared tin. Smooth the surface. Mix the sugar and cinnamon for the topping and sprinkle over the cake mixture. Dot with the butter and bake in the oven for 35 to 40 minutes until firm. Turn out and cool. Eat within four days or freeze for up to three months.

Orange Shortbread

4oz (100g) plain flour

2oz (50g) cornflour

4oz (100g) butter

2oz (50g) caster sugar

Grated rind of an orange

Caster sugar to decorate

Preheat oven: gas mark 3, 325°F, 160°C

Sieve the flour and cornflour together. Cream the butter until it is soft, then add the caster sugar and beat until the mixture is pale and creamy. Add the orange rind, then work the orange, butter and sugar into the flour mixture a tablespoon at a time. Place the shortbread mixture onto a large baking tray and roll out to an 8in (20cm) circle. Pinch the edges and prick well with a fork. Cut through into 12 sections with the back of a knife, then sprinkle with a little caster sugar. Leave to chill in the fridge for 15 minutes, then bake in a moderate oven for 35 minutes or until pale and golden brown. Cool on the baking tray for a few minutes, then lift onto a wire tray to finish cooling.

Chartwell, Kent

The house and garden of Chartwell are permeated with the memory, spirit and influence of one man who lived there for forty years. Winston Churchill – statesman, war leader and brilliant maverick politician – used the house as a refuge in times of political adversity and created the Chartwell that visitors see today.

In 1922 he bought a gloomy Victorian mansion set in a lovely combe with a wonderful view across the Weald of Kent. With the help of the architect Philip Tilden, he transformed it into a family home and surrounded himself with books, pictures and mementoes of a long life in the public eye. Here you can see his uniforms, his many medals and details of campaigns he fought in as a soldier and political battles lost and won. The house is furnished as it was in the thirties when Winston spent many years in the political wilderness. Here he waged a lonely battle to alert his country to the menace of war. Here, too, he consoled himself with writing, building walls, painting, and with the creation of the water garden which still gives visitors so much pleasure today.

In old age he came back to Chartwell. The fat orfe fish still swim in the pond where he fed them and his study, 'the heart of the house', is just as he left it in 1964.

Winston always called Lady Churchill 'my beloved Clemmie'. Her influence on Chartwell is also strong. The house is full of flowers and family photographs as she always had it. Lady Churchill was an excellent manager and I found a pile of recipes on the desk in her sunny bedroom

Chartwell
David Peacock

– amongst them this marmalade recipe, which is both good and useful as it uses dessert oranges which are available throughout the year.

Well-cooked, simple food such as steak and kidney pie, cauliflower cheese and shepherd's pie are staples of English country cooking and of the restaurant at Chartwell. Winston Churchill would definitely have approved.

Cauliflower Cheese

1 cauliflower
1 level tablespoon cornflour
½ pint (300ml) milk
1½oz (38g) butter

1lb (450g) mature Cheddar cheese, grated
Salt and pepper
Sprinkling of cayenne pepper

Preheat oven: gas mark 7, 425°F, 210°C

Boil or steam the cauliflower until just tender. Drain, cut into large chunks and put in an ovenproof dish. In a non-stick saucepan cream the cornflour with a little cold milk, pour in the balance of the milk and add the butter. Bring to the boil stirring continuously until the sauce has thickened. Add two-thirds of the cheese, season to taste with salt and pepper, and simmer gently for 5 minutes, or until the cheese has melted. Pour over the cauliflower, sprinkle the top with the remainder of the cheese and dust with cayenne pepper. Cook in a hot oven, uncovered, until the top is golden brown – approximately 15 minutes.

This dish looks pretty and special made in individual earthenware pots. It is extravagant on the cheese but is well worth it for the flavour.

Shepherd's Pie

1lb (450g) minced beef
Dripping
½ teaspoon thyme
1 bayleaf
1 large 8oz (225g) onion, sliced
8oz (225g) carrots, finely chopped

1 beef stock cube dissolved in ½ pint (300ml) water and thickened with a level teaspoon Bisto and a level teaspoon cornflour
A handful of frozen peas (optional)
Topping of mashed potato
Salt and pepper

Preheat oven: gas mark 5, 375°F, 190°C

In a saucepan fry the beef in dripping with the thyme and the bayleaf. Add the onion and carrots and fry a little longer to combine the flavours. Cream the Bisto and cornflour with a little water in a small saucepan – add the remainder of the water and the crumbled beef stock cube. Bring to the boil, stirring occasionally to prevent lumps, and pour over the meat and vegetable mixture. Simmer gently for 20 minutes and season to taste. Scatter the frozen peas on the bottom of an ovenproof dish, cover with the meat mixture and top with a nice thick layer of mashed potato. Score the top with a fork and put uncovered into the oven. Cook for approximately 30 minutes, or until brown and bubbling.

Shepherd's pie is a traditional English recipe, which is sometimes underrated. This recipe is particularly tasty and good.

Lady Churchill's Marmalade

3lb (1.4kg) sweet oranges	Water to cover
2 lemons	5½lb (2.5kg) sugar

Top and tail the oranges and lemons and slice them finely, removing any pips (but do not throw them away or the orange ends). Put in a large saucepan or preserving pan and add enough water to cover the fruit. Put the pips and ends of oranges in muslin, tie up in a bag and soak with the fruit overnight. Next day weigh the fruit and water *(not pips etc.)* and put the mixture back in the pan, with the muslin bag of pips. Simmer until tender, about 30 minutes. Meanwhile weigh out 1lb (450g) of sugar for every 1lb (450g) of fruit mixture. When the fruit is tender, add sugar to the pan, bring to the boil and boil hard until a set is obtained – about 30 minutes. Test for a set by cooling a little of the mixture on a cold plate (put the plate in the fridge first) – if a skin forms, it is ready. Put in clean warm jars – cover when cold. This marmalade doesn't keep as well as the traditional variety – but it is so delicious it is bound to disappear very fast!

Makes about nine/ten 1lb (450g) pots.

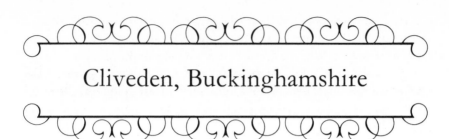

Cliveden, Buckinghamshire

High up above the Thames in Buckinghamshire stands Cliveden, an Italianate villa built in the mid 19th century and famous for its associations with power and politics and for its spectacular views over the river. It is the third house to have been built on the site. The great statesman George Canning is said to have lingered here, spending hours looking out over the Thames and its water meadows from under the ancient tree known as Canning's Oak.

The house is used as an hotel, but the visitor can stand on the immense south-facing terrace, look down on the Borghese balustrade and across the clipped conical yews and formal geometrically planted beds of the huge parterre to the river far below and the rolling hills beyond. The 1st Lord Astor, who bought the house in 1893, laid out the Long Garden and the delightful water garden with its irregular ponds full of carp, stepping stones and a pagoda. He also filled the grounds with statuary, including eight important Roman marble sarcophagi, and built the huge Fountain of Love to the north of the house.

He gave the house to his eldest son Waldorf on his marriage to Nancy Langhorne. As Lady Astor she became the first ever female member of parliament to take her seat and made Cliveden a centre of political and literary society between the First and Second World Wars.

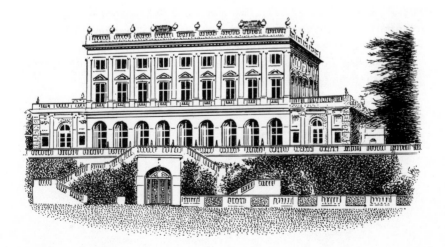

There are quieter pleasures at Cliveden now. After exploring its leafy paths and well-kept lawns and enjoying its glorious views, make your way to the east side of the house. There you will find a restaurant in the long conservatory. Geraniums and hanging baskets complete the pastoral atmosphere, perfect for a light lunch or afternoon tea. There are often unusual vegetarian dishes on the menu and hot Sunday lunches are served here.

Lentil and Vegetable Flan

8oz (225g) wholemeal pastry (made with hard margarine)

8oz (225g) split red lentils

15fl oz (450ml) vegetable stock, using 1 stock cube

1 large onion, chopped

1oz (25g) butter

1 egg

2 tablespoons chopped parsley

2 carrots, coarsely grated

2 courgettes, coarsely grated

Salt and pepper

Chopped fresh herbs to decorate

Preheat oven: gas mark 7, 425°F, 210°C

Grease and line a 9in (23cm) flan tin with the wholemeal pastry. Prick the base and bake in the oven for about 15 minutes until the pastry is set and crisp. Set the flan tin aside. Turn the oven down to gas mark 4, 350°F, 180°C. Put the lentils into a saucepan with the vegetable stock and simmer gently, stirring occasionally, until they are tender and have absorbed all the stock – about 20–30 minutes. Fry the onion in butter for a few minutes and add it to the cooked lentils, followed by the lightly-beaten egg, chopped parsley, carrots and courgettes. Mix gently until well combined, season to taste with salt and pepper, then spoon the mixture into the cooked flan case and bake in the oven for about 40 minutes – check towards the end that the mixture is not getting too dry. Decorate the cooked flan with chopped fresh herbs.

It is excellent hot or cold, and because it looks so colourful it is a good vegetarian dish in a cold buffet.

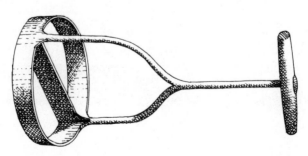

Nut and Vegetable Bake

8oz (225g) cooked brown rice

3oz (75g) brown breadcrumbs

4oz (100g) ground roasted nuts
(any non-sweetened variety will do)

1 large onion, chopped

Oil or butter

6oz (175g) carrot, coarsely grated

8oz (225g) mushrooms, chopped

Handful of chopped herbs

1 vegetable stock cube dissolved
in ½ pint (300ml) water

Salt and pepper

8oz (225g) finely-grated cheese
(optional)

Preheat oven: gas mark 4, 350°F, 180°C

Mix the rice, breadcrumbs and roasted ground nuts together in a large bowl. Sauté the onion in the fat and add to all the other ingredients. Gently mix together and season to taste. Spoon into a greased casserole dish, sprinkle the cheese on top and bake in the oven for approximately 40 minutes. It is best hot, but also good cold.

Stilton, Walnut and Celery Quiche

9oz (250g) plain flour

5oz (125g) margarine

1 teaspoon dry mustard

2–3 tablespoons cold water to
mix

Filling

6oz (175g) crumbled Stilton

4oz (100g) walnuts

3 large sticks of celery, diced

3 eggs

1 tablespoon cornflour

½ pint (300ml) single cream

Freshly ground black pepper

2 Cox's apples (or pears) for
garnish, cored, peeled and sliced
across

Preheat oven: gas mark 6, 400°F, 200°C

Grease a 10½in (26cm) quiche dish or tin. Sift the flour into a large bowl and rub in the fat using your fingertips until the mixture resembles fine breadcrumbs – add the dry mustard. Sprinkle in the cold water and draw the mixture together to form a ball. (If there is time, leave the dough to rest for 30 minutes in the fridge.) Roll out the pastry and line the greased dish. Spread the crumbled Stilton, walnuts and celery in the flan. Beat together the eggs, cornflour and cream until well combined – add black pepper to taste (no salt as the Stilton is quite salty) and fill the flan case with the mixture. Bake in the oven for 20 minutes until the top is set, then remove from the oven. Arrange the apple (or pear) slices in a circle on the quiche and return to the oven for 15 minutes more or until golden brown.

This is an excellent dish to make at the end of the Christmas holidays when the Stilton is a bit dry and the apples a bit spongy. They both taste just as good in this recipe. It is also very good substituting pears for apples.

Vegetable Curry

8oz (225g) onion, chopped

2oz (50g) butter

1 clove garlic

2 tablespoons curry paste (mild or strong according to preference)

1 tablespoon flour

1 tablespoon tomato purée

½ pint (300ml) vegetable stock (using 1 stock cube)

1 small cauliflower divided into florets

8oz (225g) carrots, peeled and sliced

4 sticks celery, sliced

1lb (450g) potatoes, peeled and cubed

2oz (50g) sultanas (optional)

1 eating apple, peeled and chopped

Salt and pepper

Garnish

2 hard-boiled eggs

2 tablespoons chopped parsley

Melt the butter in a saucepan, add the onion and garlic and cook until just soft. Stir in the curry paste, flour and tomato purée, then pour in the vegetable stock and bring to the boil stirring occasionally. Now add all the prepared vegetables, sultanas and chopped apple – season to taste and simmer very gently for about 40 minutes or until the vegetables are just cooked. Before serving, garnish with the sliced hard-boiled eggs and chopped parsley. This dish would be nice with chutney and a tomato and onion salad as an accompaniment.

Vegetarian Lasagne

2 tablespoons oil
2 onions, chopped
2 cloves garlic, crushed
6oz (175g) split red lentils
½ pint (300ml) vegetable stock
15oz (425g) tin tomatoes
2 tablespoons tomato purée
1 bay leaf
2 carrots, finely diced

2 courgettes, finely diced
¼ teaspoon each dried oregano, basil and thyme
1 tablespoon parsley
Salt and pepper
8oz (225g) green lasagne
1 pint (570ml) cheese sauce
4oz (100g) finely grated cheese

Preheat oven: gas mark 6, 400°F, 200°C

Gently fry the onions in a large saucepan. Then add the garlic, lentils, stock, tomatoes, tomato purée, bay leaf, carrots and courgettes and simmer gently for 20–30 minutes, until the lentils are tender and most of the water is absorbed. Remove the bay leaf, stir in the herbs and season to taste with salt and pepper. While the lentil mixture is cooking, prepare the lasagne. Fill a large saucepan with lightly salted water and bring to the boil. Cook the lasagne for about 8 minutes; then drain. Put a layer of lasagne in the base of a shallow ovenproof dish and cover with half the lentil mixture. Follow with another layer of lasagne, then half the cheese sauce, then the rest of the lentil mixture, finishing with a layer of lasagne. Pour over the balance of the cheese sauce and sprinkle with grated cheese. Bake for about 45 minutes, until golden brown and bubbling.

A rich full vegetarian meal. Serve with a green salad.

Corfe Castle, Dorset

The view inland from the sea on the Isle of Purbeck is dominated by the magnificent ruins of Corfe Castle. Visit it on a sunny day if you can, not as I did in a wet south-westerly gale when, like Mary Poppins, I was almost borne away by my umbrella. The views are wonderful.

William the Conqueror had a castle at Corfe of which some traces remain, but the present fortifications were only completed in the 13th century. Queen Elizabeth I sold the castle to Sir Christopher Hatton from whose daughter-in-law it was purchased in 1635 by Sir John Bankes. In the Civil War, Lady Bankes held Corfe for Charles I while her husband was away fighting: in 1642 eighty soldiers held out here for six weeks with a loss of only two men against a force who lost a hundred. Sadly, in 1646 the castle was again besieged and a band of Parliamentarians gained entry disguised as reinforcements. They forced the surrender of the castle, the rich furnishings were plundered and Captain Hughes of Lulworth was ordered to 'slight' the buildings, a task he carried out with great thoroughness.

The ruins which remain are a fascinating example of a large medieval castle, with towers, wards, great halls, courtyards and fortifications. When Corfe was owned by the Crown, national government was transacted from here if the King was in residence and a measure of its importance is that £1000 was spent on the castle during Henry III's reign from 1216–72, a massive sum at that time. Wandering round the grassy ruins, the scale of the place makes one realise how large a community must have worked and lived here, including soldiers, courtiers, pages, servants, stable boys, cooks, grooms and even farmers. During the Civil War and earlier, cattle were driven into the castle at night for safety.

At the bottom of the hill the village of Corfe, built of Portland stone, nestles below the castle. You will find an excellent National Trust shop and light lunches and teas are served in Grey Cottage just below the gatehouse. The atmosphere is cosy and old-fashioned. On chilly days there is an open fire and old prints of Corfe hang above the settles and sideboard. The setting is matched by the old-fashioned recipes, including longtime favourites such as rock cakes, chocolate sponge and fruit cake. Do try the cold ham produced on the premises. It is baked slowly covered with brown sugar – simple but mouth-watering.

Corfe Castle Rock Cakes

8oz (225g) self-raising flour	2oz (50g) sultanas
½ teaspoon nutmeg	1oz (25g) mixed peel
4oz (100g) margarine	2 eggs, beaten
4oz (100g) sugar	Milk if needed
2oz (50g) currants	

Preheat oven: gas mark 5, 375°F, 190°C

Put the flour and nutmeg into a bowl and rub in the margarine. Stir in the sugar; then mix in the fruit. Add the beaten eggs and mix to a stiffish dough, adding milk if necessary. Divide into 8 or 9 pieces and place on a greased baking sheet. Bake in the centre of the oven for about 25 minutes, until the cakes just start to brown at the edges. Cool on a wire rack.

An old-fashioned English recipe, but none the worse for that.

Jackie's Chocolate Sponge

6oz (175g) self-raising flour
1½ teaspoons baking powder
2 tablespoons cocoa powder

4oz (100g) soft margarine
4oz (100g) sugar
3 eggs

Filling

2oz (50g) butter
3oz (75g) icing sugar

2 teaspoons cocoa powder
A few drops of vanilla essence

Preheat oven: gas mark 3, 325°F, 160°C

Lightly grease and base line two 7in (18cm) round sponge tins. In a large bowl sift together the self-raising flour, baking powder and cocoa powder. Add the soft margarine, sugar and eggs and beat together – or whisk with a hand whisk – until thoroughly combined. Now divide the mixture between the two prepared tins, level off and bake in the oven for approximately 30 minutes, or until the centre of the sponge springs back into place when lightly pressed. Turn out on to a wire rack and cool.

Filling

Beat together the butter and icing sugar until light and creamy. Add the cocoa powder and a few drops of vanilla essence and continue to beat until the ingredients are well mixed.

When the sponge is cold, sandwich the two halves together with the chocolate butter icing and dust the top with icing sugar.

Do visit Corfe Castle and taste this because it is particularly good – it must be Jackie's special touch!

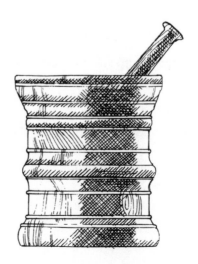

Nutmeg and Orange Fruit Cake

8oz (225g) margarine	2 tablespoons orange squash
8oz (225g) sugar	8oz (225g) currants
4 eggs	8oz (225g) sultanas
1lb (450g) self-raising flour	4oz (100g) glacé cherries
1 rounded teaspoon nutmeg	2oz (50g) mixed peel

Preheat oven: gas mark 5, 375°F, 190°C

Grease and line the bottom of an 8in (20cm) square tin. Put the margarine and sugar into a mixing bowl and beat until light and fluffy. Add the eggs one at a time, and beat well between each addition. Using a large spoon, carefully fold in the flour and nutmeg, followed by the orange squash. Gently mix in the dried fruit, then spoon the mixture into the prepared cake tin, smoothing it out evenly. Place the cake in the centre of the oven. Bake for 1 hour and then turn the oven temperature down to gas mark 3, 325°F, 160°C and cook for a further hour. Cover the top of the cake with greaseproof paper after the first hour if it is becoming too brown. Let it cool before taking it out of the tin. This cake keeps very well in an airtight tin.

The nutmeg and the orange squash are unusual in a fruit-cake recipe, but they do give it a highly individual flavour.

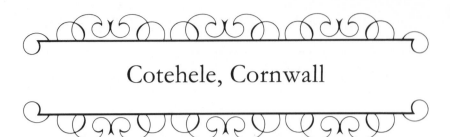

Cotehele, Cornwall

Cotehele is a jewel of a house, a remarkably unaltered medieval survival set in glorious gardens which tumble down to the banks of the Tamar, the river which divides Devon from Cornwall. The mellow stone courtyards, the Great Hall and the low-ceilinged rooms furnished with dark, polished oak furniture, tapestries and family portraits reflect the affection that Cotehele generates in all who visit or work there.

But Cotehele is not just a house. Walk down through the gardens, past the dovecote, and you will reach Cotehele Quay, where there is a tiny but delightful maritime museum. This tells the story of the great days of the Tamar a hundred years ago when the mines of Calstock and Tavistock were booming and the river was an important thoroughfare. The last of the Tamar sailing barges, the *Shamrock*, lovingly restored, is berthed here. There is a walk upstream through the Cotehele woods to the chapel built in the late 15th century by Richard Edgcumbe, or if you

go downstream you will come to the attractive group of buildings at Cotehele Mill. These include a water mill which has been put in working order, a horse-powered cider mill, a blacksmith's forge, and a carpenter's, a wheelwright's and a saddler's shop complete with their tools.

Back at the house enthusiastic cooks must not miss the old kitchen, a glimpse of a much earlier way of life. Amongst the old utensils are highly dangerous-looking Victorian 'grenade' fire extinguishers, a hot cross-bun maker, a picnic box for field workers and a small barrel for their ale. You can also read the Rules of the Kitchen in 1840, draconian by today's standards.

A copy of the rules can be bought in the shop, which is in the same great barn that houses the airy raftered restaurant decorated with farm implements and beautifully embroidered traditional smocks. Here you can eat delicious lunches and Cornish cream teas served with the traditional 'split' and drink English wine or the excellent local cider. On a cold day the soups and casseroles are a speciality and the cakes and puddings change with the season.

The Guinness cake recipe comes from the Edgcumbe Arms, which is a restaurant rather than a pub, serving lunches and teas down on Cotehele Quay.

Celery and Almond Soup

2oz (50g) butter	2 pints (1150ml) milk
1 large onion, chopped	4oz (100g) ground almonds
1 head of celery	Few drops of almond essence
1 large potato	Salt and pepper
2 vegetable stock cubes dissolved in 4fl oz (120ml) boiling water	Handful of chopped parsley and chives

Cook the chopped onion gently in butter until soft but not coloured. Chop the celery into chunks and cube the potato and add to the onion. Pour in the dissolved vegetable stock and milk and simmer until the vegetables are soft (20–25 minutes). Remove from the heat and liquidise in a blender or food processor; add the ground almonds and a few drops of almond essence and blend for a further few seconds to make a smooth soup. Season to taste with salt and pepper. Return to the heat and serve piping hot with chopped parsley and chives stirred through the soup so that it is a pretty green and white colour.

A rich soup with a delicate flavour.

Stilton and Onion Soup

2 large onions

2oz (50g) butter

2 heaped tablespoons cornflour

1 pint (600ml) milk

1½ pints (900ml) chicken stock (using 2 stock cubes)

8oz (225g) crumbled Stilton

Salt and pepper

Chop the onions finely and soften in the butter over a gentle heat. Add the flour and stir for a minute or two. Gradually pour in the milk, stirring all the time, and bring to the boil. Add the stock and simmer for 5 minutes. Remove the pan from the heat and immediately add the cheese, allowing it to melt without boiling. For a smooth texture liquidise. Season to taste and serve hot with crusty bread. It is also extremely good chilled, and makes an excellent starter for a summer dinner party.

Spiced Beef

A small amount of polyunsaturated oil

2lbs (900g) chuck steak

1lb (450g) carrots

1 large onion, sliced

½ teaspoon chilli powder, 1 teaspoon each of paprika and turmeric, 1 teaspoon mixed herbs

1 beef stock cube dissolved in 1 pint (570ml) of boiling water

14oz (397g) tin of tomatoes

1 heaped tablespoon tomato purée

1oz (25g) cornflour creamed in a little water

1½lb (700g) new potatoes

8oz (225g) frozen peas

8oz (225g) frozen sweetcorn (if you can get hold of the fresh, tiny whole sweetcorn these would be particularly delicious and pretty)

Salt and pepper

Preheat oven: gas mark 4, 350°F, 180°C

Seal the meat in the oil in a frying-pan. Place in a casserole dish with the chopped carrots. Sauté the sliced onion and stir in all the spices and mixed herbs; cook gently for a minute or two to bring out their flavour. Pour in the stock, tomatoes, potatoes, tomato purée and creamed cornflour and bring to the boil. Combine with the casserole ingredients and cook in the oven until the meat is almost tender, which should be approximately 1½ hours. Add the frozen peas, fresh or frozen sweetcorn, salt and pepper and put back in the oven until all is cooked – about a further 30 minutes.

Serve with crusty bread to mop up the spicy gravy.

This is an excellent dish to 'wait around' – just reduce the oven temperature to very low or reheat.

Elderflower and Gooseberry Fool

1lb (450g) fresh gooseberries

6oz (175g) sugar

2 tablespoons elderflower wine or cordial

½ pint (300ml) double or whipping cream

Fresh mint leaves, egg white, and caster sugar for decoration (optional)

Top and tail the gooseberries and wash them, putting them into a pan without any extra water (the juice running out of the gooseberries will provide all the liquid you need). Simmer for approximately 15 minutes, or until cooked and squashy. Add the sugar. Pour into a blender or food processor and purée. Allow to cool, then add the elderflower wine or cordial. Whip the cream until it is thick but not stiff and fold gently into *half* the gooseberry purée. Spoon the two mixtures in layers into individual glasses, starting with a layer of the gooseberry and cream mixture, then the rest of the gooseberry purée in another layer and then the remainder of the gooseberry and cream mixture. Chill before serving.

For a special occasion you could decorate the glasses with frosted leaves. Beat a little egg white, paint it on each of the mint leaves and coat with caster sugar. Leave to dry on a paper towel until crisp before decorating.

Elizabeth's Drenched Coffee Cake

Firstly, make a Victoria sandwich cake.

Victoria Sandwich (Quick Method)

4oz (100g) soft margarine

4oz (100g) caster sugar

2 eggs

4oz (100g) self-raising flour

1 level teaspoon baking powder

Preheat oven: gas mark 4, 350°F, 180°C

Line a deep 7½in (19cm) cake tin with greased greaseproof paper. Sieve the flour and baking powder together. Place all the ingredients in a mixing bowl. Beat with a wooden spoon for 2–3 minutes, or with an electric handwhisk for about one minute until the mixture is well blended. Place in the cake tin and spread level. Bake in the oven for approximately 25–30 minutes. Turn out, leave to cool and prick all over with a metal skewer.

Flavouring and Topping

½ pint (300ml) water	2 dessertspoons rum
4oz (100g) sugar	½ pint (300ml) double cream
½ cup of strong black coffee	2oz (50g) toasted flaked almonds

Put the sugar and water into a saucepan and stir over a gentle heat until the sugar has dissolved. Turn up the heat and boil fast for about 5 minutes until you have a light syrup. When the syrup has cooled, add the coffee and rum and pour over the pricked and cooled cake. Beat the cream until it just holds its shape and, using a palette knife, spread two-thirds around the sides and top of the cake. Use the remaining one-third to pipe a pretty border around the top edge of the cake and sprinkle the toasted flaked almonds in the centre. This rich pudding is a must for coffee addicts.

Guinness and Walnut Cake

8oz (225g) butter	8oz (225g) sultanas
8oz (225g) soft brown sugar	4oz (100g) mixed peel
4 eggs, lightly beaten	4oz (100g) chopped walnuts (hazelnuts or dates could be substituted)
10oz (275g) plain flour	
2 level teaspoons mixed spice	8–12 tablespoons Guinness
8oz (225g) seedless raisins	

Preheat oven: gas mark 3, 325°F, 160°C

Prepare a 7in (18cm) cake tin with greased greaseproof paper. Cream together the butter and sugar. Add the lightly beaten eggs, a little at a time, mixing well between each addition. Using a large spoon, carefully fold in the flour. Add the mixed spice, fruit, nuts and 4 tablespoons of Guinness. Turn into the prepared cake tin and smooth out evenly. Bake in the centre of the oven for 1 hour, then reduce the heat to gas mark 2, 300°F, 150°C for a further 1½ hours. Remove from the tin when cooled and prick with a skewer. Spoon over the remaining Guinness. Keep for at least one week before using. This cake will keep well for months wrapped in foil and would make an excellent Christmas cake.

Cragside, Northumberland

Cragside is the realisation of one man's dream. William Armstrong, engineer, inventor, armaments salesman and philanthropist, epitomised all that is best in the Victorian tradition. He was innovative, hard-working and romantic, but also a modest and retiring man who gave away large amounts of money to benefit his native Newcastle. He always loved the wild Northumbrian moors and bought what was to be the nucleus of his estate in Debdon Valley just outside Rothbury in 1864. In the years that followed he acquired over 1,700 acres. These he totally transformed, creating streams and waterfalls, planting firs, hemlocks, pines and sequoias on the bare hillsides, now including some of the tallest trees in Britain, and laying out woodland walks.

At Cragside the visitor can bird-watch, fish or walk in spectacular surroundings. Here, too, you can discover some of Armstrong's inventions. He designed and built an elegant footbridge in steel, the house was one of the first to be lit by electricity and a huge hydraulic ram in the basement powered the lift.

Here there are no spacious lawns or elegant flower gardens. The moors lap the house, which is built on a platform hewn out of solid cliff. Initially Armstrong built quite a modest villa, a weekend retreat for his wife and himself. But between 1870 and 1884, Richard Norman Shaw,

one of the great Victorian architects, transformed it into the magnificent gabled mansion we see today. The interiors are typically Victorian, ornate, rich and heavy. Watercolours, majolica tiles, prints and paintings abound. Much of the furniture was designed especially for Cragside, but the atmosphere is still that of a comfortable, grand but homely house – a reflection of its owner.

There is an interesting kitchen here with a hydraulically powered spit also invented by Armstrong. Cooking for visitors is done in the Vickers Rooms in the former stable block where the Visitors' Centre is housed and where there is an exhibition on Lord Armstrong's life and work.

Hearty lunches and teas are served in the wood-panelled restaurant. Northumbrian Hodgepodge Pie would satisfy the largest appetite and 'Stotties' – a white or brown flat, round loaf which is a local speciality – are served with cheese and pickle, ham and pease pudding and various other accompaniments. Cragside feasts with Northumbrian music are held on some Friday evenings in autumn, winter and spring.

Northumbrian Hodgepodge Pie

2lb (900g) stewing veal, pork and lamb in equal quantities

Dripping

8oz (225g) onions, sliced

8oz (225g) carrots, sliced

1–1½ pints (570–900ml) hot water mixed with 1 teaspoon Worcester sauce

2 tablespoons flour

2 tablespoons pearl barley

1 teaspoon mixed herbs

Salt and pepper

1lb (450g) potatoes, thinly sliced

2oz (50g) grated cheese

Preheat oven: gas mark 3, 325°F, 160°C

In a large frying-pan brown the meat, a few pieces at a time, in the dripping. Transfer the meat to a wide casserole dish. Next fry the onions and carrots for a few minutes. Stir in the flour to soak up the juices, then gradually add the hot water, stirring all the time until the liquid is smoothly blended. Pour the contents of the frying-pan over the meat in the casserole – sprinkle in the pearl barley and mixed herbs and season to taste with salt and pepper. Arrange the potato slices on top in an overlapping pattern. Cover with a lid and cook in the oven for 1½ hours. Remove the lid, scatter over the grated cheese and cook for a further 50 minutes. If the top is not browning sufficiently, turn up the oven heat for the last 15 minutes or finish under a grill.

Eccles Cakes

1lb (450g) puff pastry

Filling

8oz (225g) stale cake crumbs	½ teaspoon mixed spice
8oz (225g) jam of your choice	½ teaspoon cinnamon
8oz (225g) dried mixed fruit	Caster sugar for decoration

Preheat oven: gas mark 7, 425°F, 210°C

Grease a large baking sheet. Roll out the pastry and cut into circles approximately 4–5in (10–13cm) in diameter – this is probably easier to do if you use a saucer or something similar. Mix all the filling ingredients together until well combined and place a dessertspoon of filling onto each round. Brush the edge of each round with milk, bring up to the centre and pinch to seal well. Now turn your sealed pastry parcel over, so that the seam is underneath. Gently roll it flat to about ¼in (6mm) thick and pat it into a round shape. Place the cakes onto the greased baking sheet and cut three slits in the centre of each one. Brush them with milk, sprinkle with caster sugar and bake in the oven for about 15 minutes, or until the pastry is crisp and brown. Cool on a wire rack.

Eccles Cakes are a variation on another regional delicacy known as a Chorley Cake, and are said to have been invented by an 18th-century lady pastry cook in Eccles.

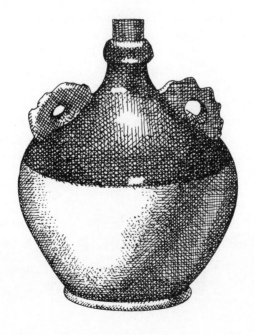

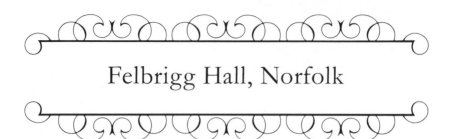

Felbrigg Hall, Norfolk

Felbrigg is approached down a long drive through fields and park. It is very much an English country house, the clear Norfolk light and keen air reminding the visitor that the North Sea is only a couple of miles away.

Robert Lyminge, architect and builder of nearby Blickling, almost certainly designed the honey-coloured Jacobean south front crowned with 'Gloria Deo in Excelsis', but the rest of the house dates from the 17th to 19th centuries. The architects who left their stamp are William Samwell, whose serene, symmetrical west wing was completed in the 1680s after his death, and in particular James Paine, who designed the east wing, rebuilt the staircase and remodelled many of the rooms in elegant 18th-century style, including the grand Gothick library. The gilded Cabinet Room, its walls lined with crimson damask, was built specially to house paintings collected by William Windham II on his Grand Tour (a peculiarly 18th-century pastime) and has magnificent plaster decoration. The garlands and swags of fruit, flowers and leaves are beautiful without being overpowering. The pretty, ungloomy bedrooms upstairs include a Chinese room which still has the original exquisite 'India' paper that Paine himself ordered, enchantingly de-corated with ducks, silver pheasants and birds of paradise.

Leave time to walk across the fields to Felbrigg church, with its fine brasses and stone and marble monuments to the Windham family who built the house and lived in it for centuries. The lovely park is also well worth exploring with its lake, orangery and ice-house, and there is a walled garden planted with fruit trees where you can sit on a warm day listening to the murmur of the white doves in the dovecote.

You eat in the old kitchen at Felbrigg. A huge dresser on one side

hung with a battery of burnished copper pans, brown check tablecloths and willow-pattern plates all contribute to the country kitchen atmosphere. The one speciality you will have to visit Felbrigg to taste is Cromer Crab Salad. Taken straight from the sea, Norfolk fishermen will tell you these are the best flavoured crabs in England. Excellent country cooking, Christmas lunches and candlelit dinners at Felbrigg are not to be missed.

Vegetarian Pie

4oz (100g) mushrooms, sliced

1 large onion, chopped

1 red and 1 green pepper, chopped

1 large leek, sliced

8oz (225g) courgettes

2oz (50g) butter or polyunsaturated margarine

9oz (250g) tin tomatoes

9oz (250g) tin kidney beans

4 tablespoons cooked brown rice

2 teaspoons yeast extract

2 teaspoons mixed herbs

1 teaspoon cornflour

Salt and pepper

2–3 cooked potatoes

2oz (50g) grated cheese

Preheat oven: gas mark 5, 375°F, 190°C

Lightly fry the mushrooms, onion, peppers, leek and courgettes in butter or polyunsaturated margarine. Add the tomatoes, beans (drained), rice, yeast extract, herbs, cornflour and seasoning and mix gently but thoroughly. Pack into a casserole, cover with sliced potatoes, top with grated cheese and bake in the oven for approximately 40 minutes or until the cheese is nice and brown. A vegetarian version of Lancashire hot-pot.

Cod in Oriental Sauce

1oz (25g) margarine

1 small onion, finely chopped

1 medium carrot, grated

$\frac{1}{4}$ pint (150ml) cider

1 teaspoon Worcester sauce

1 teaspoon mango chutney

1oz (25g) demerara sugar

1 heaped teaspoon of arrowroot blended with a little extra cider

1lb (450g) cod cut into chunks

A little chopped parsley to garnish

Melt the margarine and lightly fry the chopped onion until soft but not coloured. Then add the carrot, Worcester sauce, cider, chutney and sugar. Bring slowly to the boil so that the sugar dissolves. Add the blended arrowroot to the mixture to thicken the sauce. Lay the chunks of cod in a gratin dish and pour the sauce over them. Cover the dish and poach the fish very gently in the sauce for about ten minutes, until cooked. Take care that the chunks do not break up. Serve immediately on a bed of plain boiled rice with a scattering of chopped parsley to garnish.

Felbrigg Fish Pâté

2 dressed crabs	Grated rind and juice of 2 lemons
7oz (200g) tinned tuna fish	2 teaspoons anchovy essence
4oz (100g) peeled prawns	½ pint (300ml) single cream
6oz (175g) fresh, white breadcrumbs	Salt and pepper to taste
4oz (100g) melted butter	

Combine the flesh from the crabs with all the other ingredients. Mash well with a fork or mix lightly with a food processor and pack into ramekins. Chill and serve with chunks of fresh bread and a side salad.

At Felbrigg, this is naturally made with crab, the local delicacy, but you could substitute cooked and flaked salmon for the crab meat. You would need approximately 12oz (350g) of fish.

Sausage and Apple Plait

1lb (450g) frozen puff pastry	1 large cooking apple, peeled and thinly sliced
1lb (450g) sausage meat	1 teaspoon mixed herbs
1 large onion, finely chopped	

Preheat oven: gas mark 7, 425°F, 210°C

Roll the pastry fairly thin, into an oblong approximately 8 × 12in (20 × 30cm). Roll the sausage meat until it is 12in (30cm) long, flatten and lay along the pastry. Cover with the sliced apple, onion and herbs. Dampen the edges of the pastry and roll over. Turn the roll so that the join is underneath. Cut a cross pattern in the top, brush with beaten egg and bake in a hot oven for 20–25 minutes. Serve hot. It makes good picnic fare when cold.

Brown Betty

8oz (225g) wholemeal breadcrumbs

4oz (100g) demerara sugar

4 teaspoons mixed spice

6 large cooking apples, peeled and sliced

6oz (175g) margarine, melted

Preheat oven: gas mark 4, 350°F, 180°C

Mix the breadcrumbs, sugar and spice together thoroughly. Put a thin layer in a greased basin. Continue with alternate layers of apple and breadcrumbs, finishing with breadcrumbs. Pour the margarine over the top, cover with greaseproof paper and cook in the oven for approximately 1 hour (microwave for 10 minutes).

I always thought Brown Betty was an English dish but it is not. It is American, and was on the menu at Yale University in the 1860s!

Felbrigg Brack

12oz (350g) mixed dried fruit

1 cup dark soft brown sugar

1 cup cold tea

2 cups self-raising flour

1 medium egg, lightly beaten

Preheat oven: gas mark 2, 300°F, 150°C

Grease and base line a small loaf tin. Soak the dried fruit and brown sugar in the cold tea overnight. Add the self-raising flour and beaten egg and mix gently to incorporate all the ingredients thoroughly. Turn into the loaf tin and bake in the oven for approximately 2 hours.

Brack is an Irish word meaning speckled, probably referring to the currants traditionally used in a teabread.

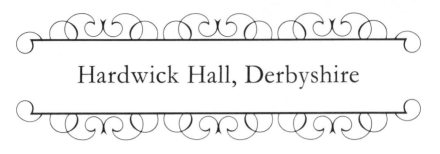

Hardwick Hall, Derbyshire

Hardwick Hall, symmetrical, golden and crowned with ES in great stone initials, is Elizabeth Shrewsbury's house. Always known as Bess of Hardwick, she was a wealthy widow of 70 when she started to build this huge house in the late 16th century. Legend has it that she mixed beer with the mortar to keep the men at work through the long, hard Derbyshire winters. Certainly her influence has not waned through the centuries. The house remains virtually as she built it, with many of the original contents listed in her inventory of 1601. The immense and awe-inspiring state rooms are unusually at the top of the house, reached by a splendid stone staircase. They are hung with tapestries and needlework pictures, some worked by Bess and her ladies. Many are very beautiful and oddly modern in colour and design. There are monumental pieces of furniture, gloomy magnificent state beds, a refectory table over 27 feet in length and Bess's solid iron jewel chest with an incredibly intricate lock opened by a surprisingly small key. The contemporary pictures include several of Mary, Queen of Scots, who was held captive at nearby Chatsworth under the guardianship of Bess's fourth husband, the Earl of Shrewsbury, after her flight to England in 1568. There are also two cushion covers worked by Mary. All these treasures enable the visitor to glimpse the life of a very grand Elizabethan family.

Outside the yew walks are tranquil, clipped and immaculate, the lawns are green carpets and huge herbaceous borders line the walls. The herb garden, one of the best in England, contains all manner of

interesting and unusual plants – lovage, orris root and opium poppies among them.

Lunches and teas are served in the old kitchen. Wooden tables are set on honey-coloured stone flags. There is a spit and the forerunner to the kitchen range – a stewing hearth – under the window. On every shelf and in ornamental patterns on the walls are hundreds of 18th- and 19th-century gleaming copper pots and pans and pewter plates, all stamped with the family crest. Steak and kidney pie and Hardwick roll are specialities. The recipe for the pie follows, but the Hardwick roll is a closely-guarded secret – you will have to visit the house to taste it!

Mrs Wilkes' Own Pork Pâté

1lb (450g) belly pork

1lb (450g) bacon bits

1lb (450g) pig's liver

1 tablespoon flour

1 tablespoon chopped onion

¼ pint (150ml) stock

Pinch of nutmeg

Herbs to taste from Hardwick garden, from your own garden, or use dried herbs

Preheat oven: gas mark 3, 325°F, 160°C

Trim the skin from the belly pork, any rind from the bacon and membrane from the liver. Cut all the meat into narrow strips about 2in (5cm) long. Fry the meat and onion briefly and pass through a fine mincer or process in a food processor. Combine all the ingredients in a large bowl and mix well. Extra seasoning is not usually necessary, but taste anyway. Place in a 2½ pint (1500ml) deep-sided earthenware dish, cover with greaseproof paper and foil and bake in a bain-marie for 1½ hours. On removing from the oven, place a plate with a weight on top until the pâté has cooled. This pâté will freeze well and is best defrosted overnight in a fridge.

Mrs Wilkes has been working at Hardwick since 1971 and bicycles to work each day over the Derbyshire hills.

Steak and Kidney Pie

1lb (450g) stewing steak

6oz (175g) kidney

1½ rounded tablespoons seasoned flour

1–2oz (25–50g) dripping

1 large onion, chopped

1 beef stock cube dissolved in ¾ pint (450ml) water

1 rounded teaspoon mustard

Salt and pepper

8oz (225g) shortcrust or puff pastry

(there are some interesting pastry recipes under Arlington Court, p.21)

Preheat oven: gas mark 7, 425°F, 210°C

Cut the stewing steak and kidney into small pieces and toss in seasoned flour. Fry the sliced onion and place in a large saucepan. Brown the meat lightly in the fat a few pieces at a time and add to the onion. Pour over the water containing the dissolved stock cube – cover and simmer gently for 1½–2 hours. Stir in the mustard and correct the seasoning to taste. Turn into a large ovenproof pie dish. Roll out the pastry and cover the pie, using any trimmings to decorate, and make a slit in the centre. Brush the top with milk and bake for 10–15 minutes. Reduce the heat to gas mark 4, 350°F, 180°C for a further 20 minutes until the pie is golden. Serve hot with green vegetables, jacket potatoes and mustard.

Microwave Lemon Pudding and Sauce

4oz (100g) self-raising flour

1 teaspoon baking powder

4oz (100g) soft margarine

4oz (100g) caster sugar

2 large eggs

Rind and juice of 2 lemons

Sauce

½ pint (300ml) water

2oz (50g) sugar

1 lemon

1oz (25g) cornflour

In a large bowl sift the flour and the baking powder. Add all the other ingredients and beat with a hand-whisk until well combined. Divide the mixture into earthenware soup bowls and microwave for 2 minutes – rest 2 minutes – microwave 2 minutes. (Cook covered in pierced cling film.) Timings would vary according to the size of the bowl and microwave power. Test to see the pudding is done. If it is, turn out and serve with the following sauce.

Sauce

Thinly peel the skin of the lemon, cut into julienne strips and blanche in boiling water. Squeeze the lemon for its juice. Boil the sugar and water in a saucepan. Cream the cornflour with a little cold water, add to the sugar mixture and bring to the boil stirring continuously. Add the blanched julienne of lemon and juice.

This is an old-fashioned recipe made in a modern way.

Chocolate Éclairs

4oz (100g) butter

½ pint (300ml) water

5oz (125g) plain flour

3 eggs

1 teaspoon sugar

Filling and Topping
6fl oz (180ml) double cream
4oz (100g) melted plain cooking chocolate

Preheat oven: gas mark 6, 400°F, 200°C

Lightly grease a large baking sheet. Put the water into a medium-sized saucepan with the pieces of butter and bring to the boil. Remove from the heat and quickly tip in the flour all at once plus the teaspoon of sugar and beat vigorously with a wooden spoon (or with an electric hand-whisk) until the paste is smooth and forms a ball that has left the sides of the saucepan clean. Let the mixture cool a little then beat in the eggs a little at a time until you have a smooth glossy paste. Spoon the choux pastry into a large nylon piping bag, fitted with a plain round nozzle ½in (1cm) in diameter, and pipe fingers 3½in (9cm) long on to the baking sheet. This should make about 12 large éclairs. Bake in the oven until well risen, crisp and golden brown. After 25 minutes slit the sides to allow the steam to escape and return to the oven for 5 minutes to dry. Not long before eating, fill with double cream and cover the tops with melted chocolate.

Hidcote Manor Garden, Gloucestershire

Without Lawrence Johnston, there would be no National Trust at Hidcote. He created Hidcote Manor Garden. When his mother bought Hidcote for him in 1907, it consisted of the house, a few fine trees, a lovely view of the Vale of Evesham, 280 acres of farmland and a tiny hamlet. There was no garden at all.

For seven years Lawrence Johnston planned and planted, creating the bones of the exquisite garden we see today. Service in the First World War interrupted his work: he was badly wounded and nearly buried alive, but afterwards he came back to his garden and repaired the results of four years of neglect. He made expeditions to China and Africa,

carrying home the rare species that flourish at Hidcote today and excite keen gardeners to make the pilgrimage to his garden. But the delight of Hidcote is that it is not just for knowledgeable enthusiasts: it will give pleasure to the most urban, ungreenfingered non-gardener.

I think the charm of the place derives partly from its scale. The garden is like a series of small interiors in the open air. Go through a wall or hedge and a new and quite different delight awaits you. The scent of the old roses in the kitchen garden is intoxicating in June, rare hydrangeas flower in August, in September the red borders are quite spectacular, and the spring bulbs and autumn foliage are both worth a special visit. If you like formality, you will appreciate the clipped hedges of the white garden, the stilt garden and the fuchsia garden. In contrast, the 'Westonbirt' area and the stream garden are luxuriantly informal.

Lunch and tea are served in the old servants' quarters of the manor. Comfortably and unpretentiously rural, one of the dining-rooms has exposed beams, unpainted stone walls and oak furniture. The excellent game pie comes from a local butcher. The pâté, hot casseroles and cakes are all made on the premises and are interesting and appetising. I was particularly taken by the carrot and banana cake – it is sticky, delicious and very nutritious, a real winner.

Courgette and Onion Quiche

8oz (225g) wholemeal pastry (made with hard margarine)

1oz (25g) butter

1 medium onion, chopped

8oz (225g) courgettes, finely sliced

2oz (50g) grated cheese

2 large eggs, beaten

½ pint (300ml) double or single cream

Salt and pepper

1 tablespoon grated Parmesan cheese

Preheat oven: gas mark 6, 400°F, 200°C

Grease and line an 8in (20cm) flan tin with the wholemeal pastry, prick the base, and bake in the oven for 15 minutes until the pastry is light brown and the base feels set and crisp to touch. Melt the butter in a frying-pan and soften the onion for a few minutes, then add the courgettes and brown them a little, turning them frequently. Transfer the onion and courgettes to the pastry case, sprinkle the grated cheese over them and pour in the beaten eggs and cream. Season with salt and pepper and sprinkle over the Parmesan cheese. Bake in the oven for 35–40 minutes, or until the centre is set and the filling golden and fluffy.

Vegetable Risotto

2oz (50g) butter

1 large onion, chopped

1 clove garlic

2 carrots, cut into chunks

2 sticks celery, cut into chunks

12oz (350g) long grain brown rice

1 pint (570ml) boiling water

4oz (100g) cauliflower, divided into florets

4oz (100g) calabrese, divided into florets

Cheese Sauce

½ pint (300ml) milk

1oz (25g) butter

1oz (25g) flour

½ teaspoon mustard

2 pinches cayenne pepper

4oz (100g) strong Cheddar cheese, grated

Heat the butter in a large saucepan. Then add the onion, garlic, carrots and celery and soften them all for about 5 minutes. Next stir in the rice. When everything is nicely coated with butter, pour in the boiling water. Put on a lid and cook gently without stirring for about 45 minutes. Meanwhile, make the cheese sauce by placing all the ingredients (except the cheese) in a saucepan and whisking them together over a medium heat until the butter has melted and the sauce thickened. Simmer gently for a few minutes, then stir in half the grated cheese. Heat some oil in a frying-pan and sauté the cauliflower and calabrese until just cooked. Finally, put the rice mixture into a large heatproof serving dish, followed by the fried vegetables; pour the cheese sauce over, then sprinkle the remaining grated cheese on top. Place the dish under a pre-heated grill until the cheese is golden and bubbling. Serve alone as a vegetarian main dish or with plain grilled meat or fish.

Hidcote Home-made Pâté

3 rashers of streaky bacon

3 fresh bay leaves

3 peppercorns or juniper berries

1lb (450g) belly of pork, coarsely minced

½lb (225g) pork liver, coarsely minced

½lb (225g) chicken liver, coarsely minced

12oz (350g) onion, minced

2 cloves of garlic

3 eggs

2oz (50g) rice flour

1 teaspoon mace

Salt, pepper, dried thyme, marjoram and chopped fresh parsley

Preheat oven: gas mark 4, 350°F, 180°C

Line a deep oblong tin with the bay leaves arranged in a fan. Then place the peppercorns in the centre of the leaves and cover them with the rashers of bacon. Stretch the rashers with a knife first to make sure they cover the bottom of the tin (but not the sides). Mix all the other ingredients together in a large bowl, season to taste with the herbs and pepper and salt. Put the mixture into the tin, smoothing the top; it should fill at least three-quarters of the tin. Cover the tin with a layer of greaseproof paper and then a layer of foil tucked in round the top. Bake for one hour in a roasting tin with water in it (deep enough to come halfway up the tin containing the pâté). Cool, and chill overnight in a refrigerator before turning out and slicing. This pâté will keep well for several days in a refrigerator. If well covered with melted lard it will keep for weeks.

Apple Pie

12oz (350g) shortcrust pastry

1½lb (700g) Bramley apples, peeled and thinly sliced

Grated rind and juice of half an orange and half a lemon

1oz (25g) soft brown sugar

¼ teaspoon ground cloves

½ teaspoon cinnamon

Caster sugar for decoration

Preheat oven: gas mark 6, 400°F, 200°C

Roll out a little more than half the pastry and line a 9in (23cm) enamel pie plate, pressing it gently and firmly all round. Cover the pastry shell with the sliced apples, sprinkling in the brown sugar, rinds, ground cloves and cinnamon between layers. Pour over the juices when finished. Roll out the other half of the pastry to form a lid. Dampen the bottom layer of pastry round the edge with water, then fix the lid into position, pressing it very firmly all round. Trim the edges and decorate the pie with any trimmings. Cut slits in the top crust to release steam and bake in a moderately hot oven for 35 to 40 minutes, or until golden brown. Sprinkle with a little caster sugar when baked. An old favourite, but the spices give it a special flavour.

Carrot and Banana Cake

8oz (225g) self-raising flour	4oz (100g) grated carrot
2 teaspoons baking powder	2 ripe bananas, mashed
5oz (125g) light soft brown sugar	2 eggs
2oz (50g) chopped walnuts	$\frac{1}{4}$ pint (150ml) corn oil

Topping

3oz (75g) soft margarine	6oz (175g) icing sugar
3oz (75g) full fat cream cheese	$\frac{1}{2}$ teaspoon vanilla essence

Preheat oven: gas mark 4/5, 350°F, 180°C

Line a 7in (18cm) round cake tin or a 2lb (900g) loaf tin with Bakewell paper. Alternatively grease and dust with flour. Sift the flour and baking powder and stir in the sugar. Add the nuts, carrot and mashed bananas and mix lightly. Lightly beat the eggs and blend into the mixture with the oil. Turn into the tin and bake for approximately 1¼ hours, or until a skewer comes out clean from the tin. Allow to cool in the tin.

Topping

Beat the ingredients together in a bowl with a wooden spoon until smooth. Spread over the cake when it has cooled.

This cake has a very distinctive banana flavour and a lovely golden colour.

Killerton, Devon

Killerton was built in 1778 by Sir Thomas Dyke Acland as a temporary residence. Altered since but now pleasantly permanent, Killerton is not a show piece in the accepted sense but a family house that many visitors can imagine living in.

The ground-floor rooms are furnished as they would have been in the 1930s. Family portraits and antiques rub shoulders with photographs, books and memorabilia of the Acland family who lived at Killerton until 1944 and still live nearby.

Costumes from the Paulise de Bush Collection are displayed upstairs on models in period settings. You might see an Edwardian family church outing, carol singers from the 1840s, a twenties party full of bright young things and a marvellously cluttered 'at home' afternoon tea of 1880. All the outfits are perfect to the smallest swansdown trim or grosgrain ribbon.

Killerton is surrounded by a wonderful garden, full of rare trees and shrubs. The huge herbaceous borders are particularly spectacular in July and August. Hidden in the grounds are a remarkable ice-house and a delightful summer-house called 'the Bear's Hut'.

The house and garden are the centre of a thriving agricultural estate and if you have lunch or tea at Killerton some of the delicious fresh vegetables and fruit will have been grown on the estate. You can eat Killerton honey with your Devonshire junket and Killerton home-made

chutney with your cheese. The bread at Killerton is famous and I'm delighted to be able to give you a recipe. But do go and enjoy the elegant dining-room, with its French windows on to the glorious garden. Soak up the atmosphere and eat the wonderful home-made luncheons, teas and high teas.

Vegetable Bake

For this dish you will need 3lb (1.4kg) of vegetables for six people – onions, carrots and tomatoes are essential, but make up the rest from the optional list given.

Onions

Carrots

Tomatoes – skinned fresh or tinned
(if tinned, do not use all the juice)

Potatoes

Aubergines

Courgettes or cucumber

Peppers

Celery

Mushrooms

Cauliflower

Leeks

6oz (175g) wholewheat pasta or 6oz (175g) green lentils

½ pint (300ml) white sauce

Grated cheese and chopped nuts

Preheat oven: gas mark 4, 350°F, 180°C

Sauté onions, carrots and potatoes in a saucepan for a few minutes just to soften slightly. Add all the other vegetables and stir – cover with a well-fitting lid and cook for a few more minutes (this combination of stir fry and steaming will not burn as there is always enough natural moisture from the vegetables and tomatoes). It is a matter of personal choice how much you cook your vegetables, but at Killerton they tend to keep them on the crisp side. Cook the wholewheat pasta in a pan of boiling water as per instructions. Make a small amount of basic white sauce – if you are using lentils make a sauce using the water the lentils were cooked in.

Mix your vegetables and cooked pasta together and put in a casserole or ovenproof dish. Pour over the sauce and sprinkle with a liberal quantity of grated cheese and chopped nuts (at Killerton they use a mixture of Brazil nuts, walnuts, peanuts and hazelnuts).

Place the dish in the oven for 20–30 minutes to heat through and brown the top.

If this is on the menu the day you visit Killerton, do try it.

Dolbury Pudding

4oz (100g) margarine	7oz (200g) chopped apples
1oz (25g) lard	7oz (200g) mincemeat
5oz (125g) soft brown sugar	8oz (225g) self-raising flour
3 eggs, beaten	A little milk if necessary

Grease a 2–2½ pint (1200–1500ml) pudding basin well and put a round of greased greaseproof paper in the base. Cream together the fat and sugar until pale and fluffy. Add the beaten eggs, a little at a time, and beat well after each addition. Stir in the apples and mincemeat and gently fold in the flour. If necessary pour in a little milk to give a dropping consistency – the mixture should be moist. Cover the basin loosely with a double layer of greaseproof paper or a piece of foil and secure with string. Place in a pan of boiling water (which should come halfway up the pudding basin) and steam for 2 hours.

Serve with any sort of fruit sauce, custard or cream.

This pudding is named after Dolbury Hill which lies behind Killerton House.

Devon Cider Cake

6oz (175g) butter or margarine

6oz (175g) soft brown sugar

3 eggs

6oz (175g) self-raising flour

2 tablespoons Devon cider (medium sweet)

Icing

½oz (13g) butter

1 dessertspoon clear honey

2½ tablespoons cider

8oz (225g) icing sugar (sieved)

6 walnut halves

Preheat oven: gas mark 4, 350°F, 180°C

Grease and line an 8in (20cm) round cake tin. Cream the butter and sugar until light and fluffy. Gradually beat in the eggs one at a time. Gently fold in the flour and mix to a soft consistency with the cider. Spoon into the tin and bake in the oven for about 50 minutes. Remove and cool.

Put the butter, honey and cider into a pan and heat gently until the butter has melted – remove from heat. Add the icing sugar and stir well. Allow the mixture to cool so that the icing becomes thicker. Pour over the cake and allow it to run unevenly down the sides. Decorate with walnuts.

A local cake using local ingredients.

Granary Bread and Rolls

Makes 3 1lb (450g) tins or approximately 15 rolls.

1¾lb (800g) granary flour

2 teaspoons salt

1oz (25g) fresh yeast or ½oz (13g) dried yeast

1 dessertspoon molasses dissolved in 3fl oz (90ml) of hand-hot water

1 pint (570ml) warm water

Put the granary flour and salt in a large bowl and warm together in the oven at its lowest temperature for a few minutes. Cream the fresh yeast with molasses and hand-hot water or sprinkle the dried yeast in and mix well. Add the yeast mixture to the warmed flour with 1 pint (600ml) of warm water; combine thoroughly but do not knead. The mixture should be very wet. Spoon into well-greased 1lb (450g) loaf tins or, for rolls, into well-greased patty tins. Prove in the oven for 15 minutes, still at the lowest temperature possible. Raise the oven temperature to gas mark 4, 350°F, 180°C and bake for 20–30 minutes for the rolls and 50 minutes for the loaves. To test if a loaf is done, turn the tin on its side, slide out the loaf and tap it on the bottom. If it sounds hollow it is cooked; if not leave it out of the tin and bake for another 10 minutes or so.

Gooseberry Chutney

2½lb (1125g) gooseberries
½ pint (300ml) vinegar
4oz (100g) raisins
4oz (100g) sultanas
1lb (450g) sugar

Pinch of turmeric
½oz (13g) black pepper, mixed spice and cinnamon combined
1 sliced onion

Boil the gooseberries in the vinegar to a pulp. Add all the other ingredients and boil until the mixture thickens, stirring frequently to prevent it catching the bottom of the pan and burning. Pot and seal.

Make this when gooseberries are cheap.

Knightshayes Court, Devon

In 1870 Knightshayes Court was described as 'stately and bold', a description that no visitor today would quarrel with. It is an imposing Victorian mansion built of red Hensley and golden Ham stone, set on a rich east Devonshire hillside two miles from the prosperous little town of Tiverton. The Heathcoat-Amory family were the biggest employers in Tiverton and in 1869 John Heathcoat-Amory, Liberal MP, sportsman and squire, commissioned the architect William Burges to build him and his family an appropriately grand house.

William Burges was an extravagant Gothic genius, a fervent medievalist more used to building churches than houses. The exterior of the house is much as he planned it, but most of the fantastic, imaginative, exotic interiors he designed were never built. By 1874 he and Squire John had fallen out and it was left to the more conservative and cost-conscious John Crace to decorate and furnish the rooms. However, some of Burges's original scheme was completed. He was responsible for the splendid stone carvings in the Great Hall, which include massive gargoyles, and the extraordinary bookcase here was also designed and painted by him (although not originally intended for Knightshayes).

John Crace decorated the house in bright primary colours, the height of fashion in 1875. Panelling and elaborate carvings abound and the dining-room frieze carries an inscription quoting from Robert Burns. As well as opulent furnishings, family mementoes and portraits, there are some fine old master paintings and a collection of 17th-century majolica.

The grounds are very beautiful – do not miss the 'garden in the wood', full of rare flowers and shrubs from all over the world.

The restaurant at Knightshayes is in Burges's old stable block, across the courtyard from the house. Good hearty casseroles, unusual soups and salads are served. Many of the cakes and puddings have local connections; the cider is brewed nearby and even the delicious white wine comes from a local vineyard.

Lentil Soup with Lemon

8oz (225g) brown lentils
3 pints (1½ litres) water
2 large onions, chopped
2 cloves garlic, crushed
2 teaspoons ground coriander
2 teaspoons ground cumin

½ teaspoon paprika
2 large carrots, chopped
1 small head of celery, chopped
Juice and rind of a small lemon
Salt and pepper

Wash the lentils thoroughly, then put all the ingredients into a large pan and bring to the boil. Simmer until everything is soft – about 1 hour. Cool slightly and liquidise in a blender or food processor. Check the seasoning and reheat. Serve with very thin slices of lemon floating on top. An unusual refreshing flavour.

Pasta Salad

½ red pepper
½ green pepper
2 stalks celery, sliced finely

8oz (225g) wholewheat pasta spirals
1 bunch spring onions

Dressing

¼pt (150ml) natural yoghurt
4 tablespoons mayonnaise
2 tablespoons salad cream

Juice ½ lemon
Salt and pepper

Add salt and a little cooking oil to a large pan of water and bring to the boil. Cook the pasta until tender – about 10 minutes. Drain well and cool. Chop the spring onions and peppers finely and add to the pasta with the sliced celery. Mix all the dressing ingredients thoroughly and coat the salad well. Chill before serving.

Spicy Bean and Potato Salad

2oz (50g) black-eyed beans

2oz (50g) mung beans

2oz (50g) pinto beans

½ teaspoon crushed coriander seed

½ teaspoon cumin powder

2 tablespoons vinaigrette

12oz (350g) new potatoes

2 large sticks of celery, chopped

¼ cucumber, peeled and diced

1 small pot of natural yoghurt

Large handful of fresh herbs to garnish

Cook the beans in plenty of unsalted water until tender. This will probably take about 1–1½ hours. If you soak the beans overnight you can halve the cooking time. Drain and dress with the vinaigrette and spices. Cook the new potatoes and allow to cool. Add the diced celery and cucumber and dress with yoghurt. Put both beans and potatoes together in a salad bowl, mix well and garnish with a handful of herbs (parsley, marjoram, tarragon and fresh coriander would all be suitable).

This salad is substantial and would make a good accompaniment to plain cold meats or as part of a vegetarian main course.

Devon Lamb in Cider

1½lb (700g) diced shoulder of lamb

2 large onions, finely chopped

Small head of celery, sliced

2 cloves of garlic, crushed

Salt

1 teaspoon paprika

1 dessertspoon cornflour and 1 dessertspoon Bisto dissolved in 2 pints (1150ml) medium dry cider

1 tablespoon dried thyme

8oz (225g) mushrooms, finely sliced

Preheat oven: gas mark 4, 350°F, 180°C

Place all the ingredients, except the mushrooms, into a large casserole dish and cook in the oven until tender – about 1½ hours. Check seasoning and add the sliced mushrooms. Return to the oven for a further 15 minutes.

Serve with rice and either vegetables or salad.

Ginger and Sultana Sponge Pudding

8oz (225g) caster sugar
8oz (225g) margarine
4 eggs
8oz (225g) self-raising flour
Pinch of salt

Vanilla essence
3 teaspoons ginger
4oz (100g) sultanas
A little milk

Preheat oven: gas mark 4, 350°F, 180°C

Grease and line a deep-sided 8in (20cm) square tin. Cream together the caster sugar and margarine until light and fluffy. Add the eggs one at a time, beating well between each addition. Gently fold in the self-raising flour and a pinch of salt. Add the ginger, sultanas and a little milk to make a soft dropping consistency. Add a few drops of vanilla essence to taste. Put in the greased tin and bake in the centre of the oven for about 30–40 minutes. Serve hot with custard or cream.

A nice old-fashioned winter pudding.

Cider Cake

3oz (75g) raisins
3oz (75g) sultanas
3oz (75g) currants
4 tablespoons cider
6oz (175g) margarine

6oz (175g) light soft brown sugar
4 eggs
8oz (225g) self-raising flour
1 teaspoon mixed spice

Preheat oven: gas mark 4, 350°F, 180°C

Soak the fruit overnight in cider.

Grease a 2lb (900g) loaf tin. Cream together the margarine and sugar until light and fluffy. Beat in the eggs one at a time, then gently fold in the flour, followed by the fruit and mixed spice. Pour into the greased loaf tin and put in the centre of the oven for approximately 70 minutes.

Another West Country recipe.

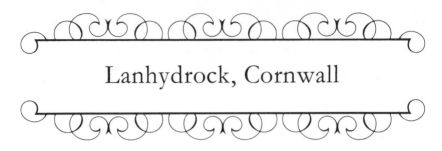

Lanhydrock, Cornwall

Built of grey Cornish granite, secure in a secluded green valley, Lanhydrock's apparently 17th-century exterior belies a much more recent building. The house was built by John, Lord Robartes just before the Civil War, and contains a magnificent 116-foot Long Gallery with an original plasterwork barrel ceiling depicting scenes from the Old Testament. Sadly, everything but the north wing which contains the gallery was destroyed in a disastrous fire on 4 April 1881. Thomas Charles, 2nd Lord Robartes of the second creation, immediately rebuilt the house to provide a family home for himself, his wife and his nine children. The Lanhydrock we see today is a remarkably preserved example of what a Victorian landowner considered necessary to pursue a modest and unostentatious life.

There is a room here for every possible occasion – there are sitting-rooms of every size, a billiard room and a smoking room for the gentlemen, a prayer room, day and night nurseries, bedrooms and dressing-rooms. The typically Victorian dining-room has dark, carved oak panelling. But there are just as many rooms beyond the green baize door as there are above stairs. An army of servants was needed to run this house, and one of the delights of Lanhydrock is that you can catch a glimpse of their lives here too.

The great kitchen was the domain of the chef, who would also preside over the cooking at the family's London house when they were there for the season. Assistant cooks, scullery maids, dairy maids and kitchen maids would work for him in the still room, dairy, dairy scullery and bake house. Great care was taken to ensure that food was cool and fresh and there are separate larders here for fish, meat and dry goods. Upstairs you can see the ironing room where valets and ladies' maids would attend to their masters' and mistresses' clothes. The huge leather suitcases and boxes in which these were packed for travelling were kept in a special luggage room and taken upstairs by a special lift. Water jugs and tidy boxes of cleaning equipment are neatly lined up in the housemaids' closet.

If all this efficiency seems too much, you can revive yourself in the restaurant which occupies the old servants' hall and housekeeper's quarters. Lunches and home-made teas feature Cornish dishes such as Lanhydrock squab pie and an Elizabethan syllabub. The delicious cider cake is taken from a recipe associated with the house.

Celery, Nut and Apple Salad

1 head of celery, sliced

3 red apples, chopped but not peeled

2oz (50g) walnuts, chopped

2oz (50g) dates, chopped (optional)

Grated lemon rind

Juice of one lemon

Salad oil

Mix the ingredients together in a bowl and pour over the lemon juice and salad oil. Combine well. A variation on a Waldorf salad.

Lanhydrock Squab Pie

Squabs were pigeons, but as these were scarce and generally eaten by the rich, lamb was substituted in the poor man's version of this dish. The apples and onions were used to make up for the lack of meat. In latter years the cream etc. has been added to enhance what is really a very tasty dish and very popular at Lanhydrock.

1½lb (700g) stewing lamb or cooked diced lamb

1lb (450g) onions, sliced

1lb (450g) cooking apples, peeled and sliced

Mixed herbs

¼ pint (150ml) vegetable stock (using a stock cube)

Salt and pepper

12oz (350g) shortcrust or puff pastry

½ pint (300ml) double cream

Preheat oven: gas mark 6, 400°F, 200°C

Arrange the meat, onions and apples in alternate layers in a pie dish. Sprinkle with mixed herbs (or just rosemary) and pour the stock over everything. Cover with the pastry and cook in the oven until the pastry is done – approximately 30 minutes. Turn the oven temperature down to gas mark 3, 325°F, 160°C and cook for a further hour. If the meat is pre-cooked, you may need a little less time. Remove from the oven and gently lift off the pastry top. Stir in the cream and adjust the seasoning. Replace the pastry lid and reheat for a further few minutes before serving.

Fruit Crumble

1–1½lb (450–700g) of fruit such as apples, plums, rhubarb etc.

Crumble Topping

4oz (100g) plain flour

4oz (100g) butter or margarine

4oz (100g) brown sugar

2oz (50g) chopped walnuts or almonds

1 teaspoon mixed spice

Preheat oven: gas mark 6, 400°F, 200°C

Layer the fruit in an ovenproof dish with sugar (the amount depending on the sharpness of the fruit).

Rub the fat into the flour until the mixture is the texture of fine crumbs. Mix in the sugar, chopped nuts and mixed spice and sprinkle on top of the fruit. Bake in the oven for 30–40 minutes.

Really delicious.

Old English Syllabub

½ pint (300ml) double cream

3fl oz (90ml) red wine

3fl oz (90ml) light ale

2oz (50g) caster sugar

Grated nutmeg

Tot of whisky (optional)

Put cream, wine, ale and sugar into a mixer and beat until thick. Do not worry if the cream separates – it will taste just as good. Fold in the whisky if used. Pour into serving glasses and put into the fridge to chill for approximately 1 hour. Sprinkle with grated nutmeg and serve with boudoir biscuits or small shortcake biscuits.

This recipe harks back to Elizabethan times when ale was used far more in cooking than it is now.

Cider Cake

4oz (100g) butter

4oz (100g) soft brown sugar

2 beaten eggs (room temperature)

8oz (225g) wholemeal flour

1 teaspoon bicarbonate of soda

½ teaspoon nutmeg

8fl oz (240ml) dry cider

Preheat oven: gas mark 5, 375°F, 190°C

Grease a 7in (18cm) cake tin, and line the bottom with greaseproof paper. Cream the butter and sugar together until light and fluffy. Sift all the dry ingredients and fold into the mixture. Add the cider slowly and beat to a soft dropping consistency. Put in the cake tin and bake for 1–1¼ hours. When cooked the cake should be springy to touch and leave the sides of the tin. When cold, store in an airtight tin for at least 24 hours before serving. It is delicious with butter and apple jelly or ginger preserve.

Little Moreton Hall, Cheshire

A first view of Little Moreton Hall is breathtaking. Surrounded by a moat containing fat carp and noisy ducks, this medieval survival is both enchanting and unbelievable. Go across the moat and enter the courtyard and you are back in the 15th century. Every part of this house is richly timbered and ornamented. Foliage patterns and trefoils abound, while crudely carved but effective warriors and beasts ·guard the gatehouse. Above the windows William Moreton's workmen have carved their own memorials: 'Rycharde Dale Carpeder made thies windows by the Grac of God'. The walls bulge at impossible angles – a Tudor Moreton added a fashionable long gallery to the two-storey hall and the strain has pulled the structure out of shape. But fortunately for us the house is still standing and for an hour or two the visitor can experience a taste of life in a medieval country house.

Little Moreton Hall is an empty house. It contains three original pieces of furniture, but since so little of the period survives, the Trust has not attempted to simulate a domestic interior. However, the rooms are well explained in the guidebook and it is well worth taking one of the guided tours which operate from time to time if you have the opportunity. They really bring the house alive. The Great Hall, the hub of medieval life, is the earliest part. Do not miss the painted wall frieze of Susanna and the elders with colours that still glow in the Parlour and the

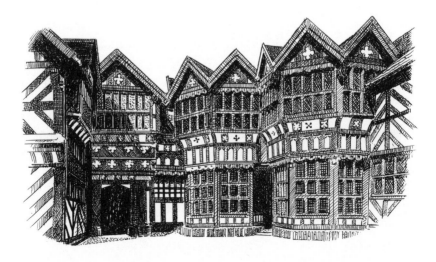

huge wood corbels in the guests' hall. In the Long Gallery it is possible to see the roof construction, curved braces morticed and tenoned into the rafters, both beautiful to look at and effective. Notice, too, the fine plasterwork at each end. There are two original garderobes set in their own tower, the contents of which would have been dug out and used as fertiliser. Services are still held in the small, simple chapel.

Home-made teas are served in the old buttery off the hall. The room is small and intimate, there is waitress service and on cold days a fire crackles in the corner stove. Medieval life must have been cold, draughty, smokey and uncomfortable, but now you can enjoy the atmosphere of the Middle Ages while sampling the pleasures of the 20th century – a pot of tea, a good old-fashioned scone, and a piece of fruit cake or fruity gingerbread!

Fruity Gingerbread with Wholemeal Flour

4oz (100g) butter or margarine	4oz (100g) wholemeal flour
4oz (100g) soft brown sugar	2 teaspoons ginger
4oz (100g) black treacle	2 teaspoons cinnamon
1 beaten egg	1 teaspoon bicarbonate of soda
$\frac{1}{4}$ pint (150ml) warm milk	2oz (50g) mixed dried fruit
4oz (100g) plain flour	

Preheat oven: gas mark 2, 300°F, 150°C

Grease and line an 8in (20cm) square cake tin. Melt the butter, sugar and treacle in a saucepan – cool and add the beaten egg and warm milk. Sift the flours, spices and bicarbonate of soda together in a mixing bowl and add the mixed dried fruit. Make a well in the centre of the dry ingredients, pour in the treacle mixture and beat very thoroughly. Pour into the tin and bake in the oven for 1 hour.

A lovely old-fashioned gingerbread.

Mrs Middlemiss's Rich Fruit Cake

—

4oz (100g) caster sugar

4oz (100g) dark brown soft sugar

8oz (225g) soft margarine

2oz (50g) treacle

4 eggs

3oz (75g) self-raising flour

7oz (200g) plain flour

1 tablespoon mixed spice

1½lb (700g) mixed dried fruit

1 tablespoon milk

Preheat oven: gas mark 2, 300°F, 150°C

Grease and line an 8in (20cm) square cake tin. Cream together the sugars, margarine and treacle and add the eggs one at a time, beating well between each addition until well combined. Sift the flours and mixed spice into a separate bowl, add the dried fruit and mix together. Gradually fold into the creamed mixture and finally add the milk. Spoon the mixture into the cake tin and bake in the centre of the oven for 2½–2¾ hours.

Mrs Middlemiss's fruit cake is worth a detour.

Little Moreton Hall Cookies

—

5oz (125g) butter or margarine

4oz (100g) caster sugar

1 beaten egg

2oz (50g) chocolate chips, or chopped hazel nuts, or chopped glacé cherries

8oz (225g) self-raising flour

Preheat oven: gas mark 4, 350°F, 180°C

Grease two large baking sheets. Cream the fat and sugar until pale and fluffy. Add the egg and beat well. Stir in the chocolate chips (or nuts, or cherries) and the flour and mix to a fairly firm dough. Knead lightly, then place in a polythene bag and chill for 30 minutes until firm. Either make into a roll and cut into slices ¼in (6mm) thick or roll out to ¼in (6mm) thick on a lightly floured surface and cut into rounds with a 2½in (6cm) fluted cutter. Put on the baking sheets and bake for about 10–15 minutes until firm and very light brown in colour.

Crisp and delicious.

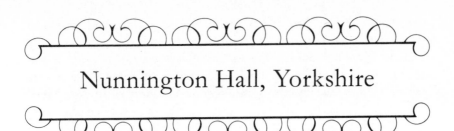

Nunnington Hall, Yorkshire

Nunnington Hall stands in a green valley beside the River Rye, the Vale of York to the south, the Yorkshire Moors to the north. Built of tranquil, honey-coloured stone with elegant but not forbidding proportions, the house seems very much at home in its setting. Sheep graze peacefully beyond the wrought-iron gates.

Nunnington has had a chequered past. The owners of the Hall persistently backed the losing side under the turbulent Tudors and Stuarts. The house was altered, neglected and restored and there are tales of a sad ghost, but the atmosphere is warm and welcoming, with a tangible feeling of affection. Panelling glows in the south-facing oak hall, setting off the splendid chimney-piece. Magnificent tapestries hang at either end of the drawing-room and also at the head of the great staircase. The tiny oratory is a reminder that the family remained Catholic during very troubled religious times, and several members were imprisoned in the Tower of London for their beliefs.

The rooms at Nunnington display mementoes and treasures associated with the house and its owners over several centuries. Some are curious, such as the lowering animal heads shot by Colonel Fife in the 1920s. Some are beautiful, such as the exquisite four-poster bed and a wonderful painted ceiling in Lord Preston's room.

The top floor houses the Carlisle Collection, miniature period rooms

furnished with tiny perfect replicas of furniture, china and glass, and even musical instruments in working order.

Do leave enough time to take tea in what were the family's sitting- and dining-rooms, or on fine days in the sheltered riverside tea garden where you can share your crumbs with ducks and moorhens. Freshly baked Yorkshire specialities such as Yorkshire parkin and wholemeal scones with Wensleydale cheese are on the menu. Those in the know return again and again!

Nunnington Spiced Fruit Loaf

4fl oz (120ml) water	4fl oz (120ml) cold milk or water
4oz (100g) margarine or butter	4oz (100g) self-raising flour
6oz (175g) granulated sugar	4oz (100g) plain flour
12oz (350g) mixed dried fruit	1 rounded teaspoon mixed spice
1 teaspoon bicarbonate of soda	2 eggs, beaten

Preheat oven: gas mark 3, 325°F, 160°C

Grease a 2lb (900g) loaf tin. Put the water, margarine or butter, sugar and mixed dried fruit in a heavy-based large saucepan. Boil together for 1 minute and then add the bicarbonate of soda. Leave to cool and then stir in the cold milk or water. Sift the flours and mixed spice into a mixing bowl and make a well in the centre. Pour in the beaten eggs and all the ingredients from the saucepan and mix well with a wooden spoon. Pour into the loaf tin and bake for 45 minutes to 1 hour till risen and brown. Cool slightly before turning out onto a wire rack to cool further.

Yorkshire Parkin

8oz (225g) butter or margarine

8oz (225g) golden syrup

4oz (100g) self-raising flour

4oz (100g) wholemeal flour

4oz (100g) rolled oats

4oz (100g) oatmeal

8oz (225g) sugar

1 heaped teaspoon ground ginger

½ teaspoon baking powder

1 egg beaten and made up to
6fl oz (180ml) with milk

½ teaspoon salt

Preheat oven: gas mark 3, 325°F, 160°C

Thoroughly grease an 8in (20cm) square cake tin. Melt the butter and golden syrup together in a saucepan. Mix all the dry ingredients together in a mixing bowl and stir in the melted ingredients. Add the egg and milk and thoroughly combine using a wooden spoon. Pour into the well-greased tin and bake in the oven for approximately 45 minutes. Remove from the tin whilst still slightly warm to avoid sticking. The parkin will keep very well in an airtight tin or will freeze.

Parkin is traditionally kept in a tin with a sliced Cox's apple to keep it damp, and left to mature for at least a week.

Gingerbread People

4oz (100g) margarine

3oz (75g) golden syrup

12oz (350g) self-raising flour

1 teaspoon ground ginger

4oz (100g) sugar

1 egg, beaten

Raisins for eyes and buttons

Metal or plastic gingerbread
people cutters

Preheat oven: gas mark 4, 350°F, 180°C

Melt the margarine and golden syrup together. Sieve the dry ingredients together, add the melted margarine and syrup and beaten egg. Knead until smooth. Chill for 30 minutes. Roll out ¼in (6mm) thick and cut into gingerbread men and women. Lay on baking sheet. Put in eyes and buttons. Bake 10–12 minutes. Makes approximately 12 people.

Penrhyn Castle, Gwynedd

Penrhyn Castle is monumental. It lies among spectacular scenery overlooking Anglesey and the Menai Straits with Snowdonia and its dark mountains glowering behind, but still succeeds in dominating these awe-inspiring surroundings. G. H. Dawkins Pennant, later 1st Lord Penrhyn, would have been deeply satisfied with the effect his house has on 20th-century visitors. It was he who commissioned Thomas Hopper in 1820 to build a 'Norman' castle on a vast scale, financed with the profits from the Penrhyn slate quarries which he owned.

Approaching the huge pile is enough to subdue any visitor, and from the moment you enter the Great Hall, you cannot but feel that grandeur on a massive scale is what the architect was aiming for. The reception rooms are extraordinary – ornate, magnificent and enormous. The 'Norman' furniture specially designed for the house is heavily carved, splendidly solid and very uncomfortable. It is easy to imagine the grandest Victorian house parties enjoying whist, bezique and gossip in the drawing-room, billiards in the library, and eating enormous meals off crystal and Minton in the dining-room, sombrely observed by the old master paintings collected by the 1st Lord Penrhyn.

Upstairs there are miles of corridors, warrens of staircases, gloomy bedrooms and dressing-rooms and a chapel where the family and house-guests went for compulsory morning prayers. They would be warmed by an open fire in the gallery while the servants shivered piously in the pews below. There are some wonderful beds: a brass four-poster made

for Edward VII when Prince of Wales, hung with an exquisite fabric designed by William Morris; an alarming slate bed weighing over a ton, and a suitably ornate oak four-poster which Queen Victoria slept in.

Naturally it required an army of servants to run this household in a suitably grand manner. There are 52 bells in the corridor behind the Butler's Pantry and a lad was employed full time simply to stand and watch which bell rang and then to summon the appropriate servant.

The housekeeper's room off the bell passage is now the tea-room, where you can also eat good home-made soup at lunch time. If it is tea-time, Welsh cakes are a delicious alternative to scones and coconut shortbread is very popular. Thus refreshed, do visit the doll and railway museums in the stable yard.

Green Pea and Mint Soup

1¼lb (550g) frozen peas

1 teaspoon dried mint (or fresh if available)

1½ pints (900ml) chicken stock

1 medium onion, chopped

2oz (50g) butter

Double cream to decorate

Place the peas, mint, chicken stock and onion in a large saucepan, bring to the boil and simmer gently for 20 minutes. Liquidise in a blender or food processor with the butter. Serve either hot or cold with a swirl of cream.

A beautiful colour and a lovely delicate flavour.

Lentil Soup

4oz (100g) red lentils

1oz (25g) butter

1 onion, peeled and chopped

2 large carrots, chopped

2 sticks celery, sliced

1½ pints (900ml) chicken or ham stock

1 teaspoon dried thyme

Salt and pepper

Chopped parsley

Melt the butter in a large saucepan and fry the onion for a few minutes but do not brown it. Add the other vegetables and cook gently for 5 minutes, stirring often to prevent sticking. Mix in the lentils and stir for a minute or two so that the lentils get coated with the butter; then put in the stock and thyme. Bring the mixture to the boil, cover it and leave to simmer for about 1 hour or until the lentils are tender. Liquidise in a blender or food processor. Adjust the seasoning, reheat and serve with a sprinkling of chopped parsley.

Welsh Cakes

8oz (225g) self-raising flour	3oz (75g) caster sugar
Pinch of salt	3oz (75g) currants
Pinch of mixed spice	1oz (25g) chopped peel
Pinch of cinnamon	1 egg
4oz (100g) margarine	Milk to bind

Preheat and grease a griddle or heavy-based frying-pan. Sift together the flour, salt and spices and rub in the fat until the mixture resembles fine breadcrumbs. Stir in the sugar and the fruit. Mix with the egg and milk to a firm but not dry dough. Roll out to $\frac{1}{4}$–$\frac{1}{2}$in (6–12mm) thick and cut into rounds. Cook on a moderately hot griddle till brown on both sides – about 10 minutes in all.

A local recipe – serve hot dusted with extra caster sugar or cold with butter.

Coconut Shortbread

4oz (100g) butter	5oz (125g) plain flour
2oz (50g) sugar	Pinch of salt
2oz (50g) desiccated coconut	

Preheat oven: gas mark 4, 350°F, 180°C

Grease a baking sheet. Mix the butter and sugar in a food processor until smooth and creamy. Add the desiccated coconut, flour and salt and continue to blend until the mixture forms a ball around the blade. Roll out on a lightly floured surface to about $\frac{3}{4}$in (2cm) thick. Cut into fingers, prick with a fork and place on the baking sheet. Bake in the oven for about 20–25 minutes or until pale gold. When cool, dredge with caster sugar.

A variation on a National Trust tea-room favourite.

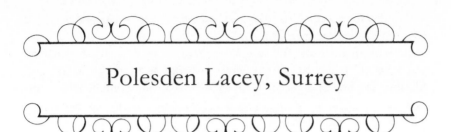

Polesden Lacey, Surrey

Strikingly situated on high ground with a fine view south to the Downs, Polesden Lacey is a two-storey 'Regency villa' designed by Thomas Cubitt in 1821. Although altered since then, the exterior still has a strong Regency flavour, but inside it is unmistakably the house of a great Edwardian hostess, the Honourable Mrs Ronald Greville. A formidable lady with a powerful personality, she entertained all society from royalty downwards here, before and after the First World War. Beverley Nichols, Osbert Sitwell and Harold Nicolson all stayed at Polesden Lacey and commented on her acid wit and sharp tongue, but politicians were her favourites.

The rooms are opulent, the furniture ornate, the china which she loved is magnificent. There are important collections of Chinese, Meissen and Fürstenberg porcelain and 16th-century majolica. In the dining-room, laid for dessert, you can read the elaborate menu served at dinner. It is easy to imagine 'Mrs Ronnie' in the sunny study built on by the Grevilles organising her army of servants for the next great house party.

In Mrs Greville's heyday the gardens were an essential part of the organisation, providing not only the perfect backdrop to the house but also flowers for the rooms and fruit and vegetables for the kitchen. Before the First World War there were forty gardeners. In the greenhouses strawberries were grown out of season and violets, bred to flower in November, caused a sensation. Sadly the greenhouses are no more, but the gardens still provide a beautiful setting for the house. The walled garden and herbaceous borders contain many interesting plants

and there are specialist iris, rose and lavender gardens. Farther afield are shady walks and mature trees.

Farther afield too is the restaurant, housed in what used to be the stable block. It is a long light room restfully decorated in beiges and browns. At one end the original looseboxes now contain tables and benches, at the other there is a wonderful display of unusual salads and calorific cakes and puddings. Hot dishes are always available and hot puddings such as apple and sultana sponge go down a treat. The truffle triangle Mrs Thomas makes owes its inspiration to Cranks but her touch has made it especially her own. It is rich, wickedly fattening and irresistible – definitely worth a detour.

Cheese and Lentil Loaf

1 tablespoon oil	$\frac{1}{4}$ pint (150ml) water
1 large onion, sliced	2oz (50g) mushrooms, chopped
8oz (225g) red lentils	2 eggs, beaten
2 level tablespoons diced red or green pepper	4oz (100g) grated Leicester cheese
2 tablespoons coarsely grated carrot	4oz (100g) fresh brown breadcrumbs
14oz (400g) tin of tomatoes	2 level teaspoons dried thyme
1 teaspoon tomato purée	Salt and pepper

Preheat oven: gas mark 4, 350°F, 180°C

Grease a 2lb (900g) loaf tin thoroughly. Heat the oil in a large saucepan and fry the onion until soft. Add the lentils, peppers, carrots, tomatoes with their juice, tomato purée and water. Bring to the boil and simmer for 30 minutes, or until the lentils are soft. Allow to cool slightly. Stir in the mushrooms, eggs, cheese, breadcrumbs and thyme and salt and pepper to taste. Mix well and spoon into the loaf tin. Bake in the oven for 1 hour. This can be served either hot or cold.

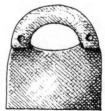

Carrot and Orange Salad

8oz (225g) coarsely grated carrot
1 orange, peeled and chopped
2oz (50g) flaked almonds

Juice of 1 lemon
2 tablespoons clear honey
Salt and pepper to taste

Gently combine the grated carrot, orange pieces and flaked almonds. Whisk the lemon juice and clear honey together with a fork and season with salt and pepper. Pour over the salad ingredients and once again mix with care.

Mushroom and Mixed Pepper Salad with Soy Sauce

1lb (450g) very fresh button mushrooms
1 red pepper
1 green pepper
3 tablespoons vinaigrette dressing

1–1½ tablespoons soy sauce
1 tablespoon chopped chives
1 tablespoon chopped parsley

Slice the button mushrooms finely. De-pip and slice the peppers finely. In a large mixing bowl combine the vinaigrette and soy sauce and nearly all the chives and parsley (reserve a little to scatter on top of the salad). Toss the vegetables in the mixture and serve in a shallow dish garnished with parsley and chives.

Colourful and unusual!

Apple and Sultana Sponge

1lb (450g) cooking apples
1 or 2 tablespoons water
2oz (50g) brown sugar
2oz (50g) sultanas
½ level teaspoon cinnamon

1 level teaspoon cornflour dissolved in a little water

Sponge cake mixture
(use the sponge recipe on p.93, omitting the ginger)

Preheat oven: gas mark 4, 350°F, 180°C

You will need a well-greased, deep-sided, square or rectangular cake tin. Peel, core and thickly slice the apples and put in a saucepan with a little water and the brown sugar. Cook gently until the apples are just starting to disintegrate. Add the sultanas, cinnamon and cornflour and heat until the juices start to thicken slightly. Pour this mixture into the bottom of the cake tin and spread evenly. Make up the sponge cake mixture and spread on top of the apple. Bake in the oven for 30–40 minutes and then turn out onto a large serving dish. Cut into wedges and serve with lashings of cream!

Chocolate Truffle Triangle

1½lb (700g) cake crumbs or trifle sponge

4oz (100g) mincemeat or marmalade

2oz (50g) chopped walnuts

2oz (50g) cocoa

6oz (175g) chocolate (plain chocolate dots or Meunier chocolate would be suitable)

3–4 tablespoons brandy (or orange juice, rum etc.; the amount of liquid needed will vary according to the type of cake crumbs used – a firm consistency is required)

3oz (75g) soft margarine

Crumble the cake or trifle sponge with your fingers in a large mixing bowl, or use a food processor if you have one. Add the mincemeat, chopped walnuts, cocoa powder and liquid and work together to make a smooth but firm consistency. Turn the mixture onto a work surface and form into a triangular log shape with your hands. Place on a wire rack and refrigerate for a couple of hours. Gently melt the chocolate and margarine in a small saucepan and allow to cool until it is starting to thicken. Spread carefully over the triangle using a palette knife and leave to set. If any chocolate has fallen through the wire rack it can be gathered up and reheated. Repeat the covering process once more. Serve cut into slices.

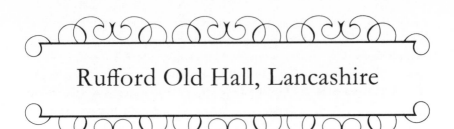

Rufford Old Hall, Lancashire

Rufford Old Hall is a series of surprises. Coming up the drive, you are immediately faced by the Great Hall. Half-timbered, with a huge bay window, it is one of the best examples of a 15th-century hall in England. But the wing at right-angles to it on the left is a pleasant Charles II house, almost cosily domestic. It has mellow red brickwork, white-painted windows and the date 1662 above the door. Walk the other side of the hall and you are brought up short by the castellated towers and chimneys of the additions made in 1821, which link the Great Hall with the Carolean wing. A further surprise is that this hotchpotch forms such a harmonious and pleasing whole!

There are puzzles inside as well. Rufford's treasure is the Great Hall, which is magnificently medieval and dominated by the richly-carved movable wood screen. This is one of only three still surviving in England, and it must have taken an army of strong men to move it; its pinnacles tower above the visitor. Legends abound here, including a tradition that Shakespeare performed in the hall. In the void behind the

curve of the roof at the high-table end of the room is a secret chamber. Was this used during Elizabeth I's reign when the Hesketh family clung to their Catholic faith and a cousin was executed at St Albans for plotting against the queen? Above the hall is the drawing-room, furnished in early Victorian style. It has a spy-hole into the hall ingeniously disguised behind a door, but no-one knows the date of the room. The roof timbers and the spy-hole suggest it is 16th-century, but the windows indicate it is contemporaneous with the other 1821 alterations.

In addition to these teasing questions there is the Rufford village museum. Here you can see a fascinating display of everyday items from the 19th century, including a copper still, a penny-farthing bicycle, eel knives, a cheese press, a man trap, and beautifully-preserved Victorian costumes and dolls. There are rare bees and bats in the roof and the possibility of a glimpse of the even rarer red squirrel in the beautifully laid out gardens. A visit to Rufford is undoubtedly a must.

Home-made lunches and teas are served in two delightful small tea-rooms with stone flags, oak furniture and blue-and-white china and linen. Polished pewter and interesting old storage jars line the shelves and there is a black-leaded range in the old kitchen. Mrs Beddows, who presided over the kitchen for 16 years, has just retired. Her jams are famous and I have included two of her recipes, but I am also very happy to confirm that the tradition of good home cooking will continue.

Walnut Biscuit Cake

8oz (225g) digestive biscuits	1 beaten egg
4oz (100g) butter or margarine	2oz (50g) chopped walnuts
5oz (125g) light brown sugar	Few drops of vanilla essence

Butter icing

2oz (50g) butter	1 tablespoon milk or warm water
4oz (100g) icing sugar	Halved walnuts to decorate
Few drops of vanilla essence	

Grease a 7½in (20cm) flan tin. Break the digestive biscuits into small pieces and place in a large bowl. Melt the butter or margarine in a saucepan, add the sugar and beaten egg and mix until the sugar has dissolved. Stir well and cook until the mixture bubbles for one minute. Add the nuts and vanilla essence and pour over the broken biscuits. Mix until the biscuits are well coated. Press into the greased tin with the back of a spoon and leave to set.

Butter icing

Cream the butter until soft and gradually beat in the sugar, adding a few drops of vanilla essence and then the milk or water. Turn out the biscuit cake, cover with the butter icing and decorate with halved walnuts.

This biscuit cake is very rich – serve slightly chilled.

Blackberry and Apple Jam

2lb (900g) blackberries	12oz (350g) cooking apples
½ pint (300ml) water	(prepared weight)
	3lb (1350g) sugar

Pick over and wash the blackberries, put them in a pan with ¼ pint (150ml) of water and simmer slowly until soft – sieve to remove the pips. Peel, core and slice the apples and add the remaining ¼ pint (150ml) of water. Simmer slowly until soft and make into a pulp with a spoon or a potato masher. Add the blackberry purée and sugar, bring to the boil and boil rapidly, stirring frequently, until setting point is reached. Test for a set by cooling a little of the mixture on a cold plate (put the plate in the fridge first) – if a skin forms, it is ready. Pot into warm jars and cover.

Marrow and Lemon Jam

2lb (900g) marrow (prepared weight)

2lb (900g) sugar

Thinly peeled rind and juice of 2 lemons

Peel the marrow, remove the seeds and cut into pieces about ½in (12mm) square. Place in a basin, sprinkle with the sugar and allow to stand overnight. Tie up the lemon rind in a piece of muslin and place in a large, heavy pan with the marrow, sugar and lemon juice. Simmer until the sugar has dissolved, then boil until setting point is reached (see above) and the marrow looks transparent. Remove the muslin bag, pot into warm jars and cover.

Rhubarb Chutney

2lb (900g) rhubarb	1 teaspoon mixed spice
8oz (225g) onions	1 teaspoon ground pepper
1½lb (700g) brown sugar	1 teaspoon ground ginger
8oz (225g) raisins	1 teaspoon salt
½oz (13g) mustard seeds	1 pint (570ml) vinegar

Cut the rhubarb into 1in (2.5cm) lengths and chop the onions finely. Put all the ingredients into a large heavy pan and simmer gently, stirring frequently until the mixture is of a thick consistency (like jam) with no excess liquid. Put into warm pots and cover tightly.

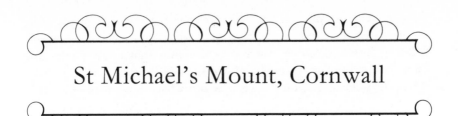

St Michael's Mount, Cornwall

A first view of St Michael's Mount is breathtaking. The castle and church appear to rise sheer from the sea. It is easy to believe the many myths and stories which surround this rocky island just off the far south-western tip of Cornwall.

St Michael's Mount has been a refuge, a place of pilgrimage and a sanctuary for a thousand years and before that it was a flourishing port during the Roman occupation of Britain. It has been a Benedictine priory, a fortress and finally a home for the St Aubyn family. It was besieged in the Wars of the Roses, captured by Cornish rebels in 1549 and in 1588 the beacon on the summit signalled the first sighting of the Spanish Armada as it entered the English Channel. Sir Francis Basset's wife held it as a Royalist stronghold during the Civil War. He wrote her poignant letters full of concern and worry which are on show in the museum. Reading them takes you back 400 years and brings the war immediately to life. Colonel John St Aubyn purchased the Mount from the Basset family in 1659.

Climb the steep stone steps to the castle and see how snug and impregnable it still feels – as any good castle should. I defy anyone to see where the old castle stops and Victorian additions begin. There are lovely contrasts inside. The church is medieval and services are still held here. The room known as Chevy Chase was originally the refectory of the monastery. It has a splendid 17th-century table and takes its name from the plaster frieze of energetic huntsmen round the walls. The Armoury is 16th-century and the elegant Gothic Blue Drawing-Rooms were decorated and furnished in the 18th century.

You can walk to the Mount at low water, across a stone causeway

built by William Morton, the first Archpriest. He also built the little harbour with the cottages clustered round it, one of which contains the Sail Loft Restaurant. Cheerful and light with gingham tablecloths and views across the bay, lunches and teas include the most delicious fish. What you get depends on the weather and what the boats have landed, but everything is as fresh as you will ever find it. I particularly enjoyed the seafood pancakes – the inclusion of crab gives them a typically West Country flavour. The lemon cheesecake is a classic and this is an excellent recipe.

Seafood Pancakes

Mixture for 6–8 pancakes depending on the size of the pan.

3oz (75g) plain flour	1 small egg, whisked
Pinch of salt	1 tablespoon (15ml) vegetable oil
4fl oz (120ml) water	½oz (13g) butter
4fl oz (120ml) milk	

Sieve the flour and salt into a bowl. Mix all the liquid ingredients and whisk into the flour. Leave to stand for 1 hour. Pour approximately 2fl oz (60ml) of the mixture into a hot, oiled 8in (20cm) pan. Leave until the bottom bubbles (approximately 1 minute) – loosen and turn over to cook the other side.

The pancakes can be made in advance and stored with greaseproof paper between them in the refrigerator for four days, or in the freezer for a month.

Seafood Mix

12oz (350g) cooked white fish, e.g. cod, haddock, whiting, conger	2oz (50g) mushrooms, sautéd with a little onion
2oz (50g) brown (cream) crab meat	Few sprigs parsley
	Pinch of basil
2oz (50g) white crab meat	Salt and pepper
(Brown and white crab meat is available in tins or frozen, but fresh is best)	½ pint (300ml) white sauce
	⅓ cup dry white wine

Mix all the ingredients (except the wine and parsley) with a little of the white sauce and season to taste. Divide the mixture between the pancakes and roll up. Add the white wine to the balance of the white sauce and use to coat the filled pancakes. If necessary, reheat until the sauce is bubbling. Garnish with chopped parsley or chopped spring onions. Serve with vegetables or a green salad.

Lemon Cheesecake

3oz (75g) Cornish butter

6oz (150g) crushed biscuits (digestive or any other)

5 leaves of gelatine (or two 1oz (25g) sachets of powdered gelatine)

8oz (225g) full fat cream cheese

Juice and zest of a lemon

5fl oz (150ml) soured cream

3oz (75g) caster sugar

2 eggs, separated

2fl oz (60ml) whipped cream

Melt the butter in a small saucepan and add the crushed biscuits. Press the mixture down firmly into an 8in (20cm) spring release tin or loose-bottomed cake tin. Chill for 2–3 hours. Melt the gelatine in 2 tablespoons of boiling water. Mix together the cream cheese, juice and zest of a lemon, soured cream, caster sugar and egg yolks. Whisk the egg whites until stiff. Using a separate bowl, whisk the cream until stiff. Fold the egg whites and cream into the cheese mix. Add the melted gelatine, pour into the tin and chill overnight.

Decorate with more whipped cream and lemon segments.

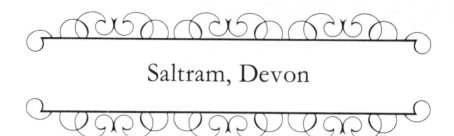

Saltram, Devon

Saltram is a dove-grey stucco mansion built by the Parker family in 1740 round a much older house. It stands in an elegant park on the banks of the River Plym in south Devon. Robert Adam designed the Saloon and the Dining-room down to the last detail of the door knobs, and very beautiful they are, but the visitor to Saltram can experience an essentially 18th-century atmosphere in *every* room. The sumptuous plaster ceilings date from 1740. The pictures in the Morning Room are hung triple banked in the fashion of the day. John Parker, Lord Boringdon, was one of Joshua Reynold's greatest friends and twelve of his pictures hang in the house, including a delightful study of Lord Boringdon's children. It is certain, too, that Reynolds helped his patron and friend to form the splendid picture collection. Most of the furniture is 18th-century and much of it is mentioned in old inventories of the house.

Upstairs is the charming Chinese Chippendale Bedroom which reflects the 18th-century fashion for collecting and imitating oriental furnishings. This is matched by the spectacular Chinese Dressing-Room, with its particularly fine exotic wallpaper. In the grounds are a little temple called Fanny's Bower, a pretty orangery, and a little octagonal folly called the Castle. The amphitheatre on the banks of the Plym has seats hewn from the rock and was a popular place for picnics. These features reflect the 18th-century enthusiasm for pastimes in the open air and the contemporary interest in Classical architecture.

The Great Kitchen was built after a fire in 1778. It is a wonderful room complete with an open range and all kinds of kitchen utensils,

including six hundred copper pans and moulds. The cockroach catchers are a salutary reminder of a less hygienic age.

The original kitchen is now the restaurant at Saltram and is reached from the garden room across a small pretty courtyard. The room is homely and welcoming with stone flags on the floor and a large dresser on which appetising cakes are displayed. Saltram shortbread is famous, but the recipe is a secret! Lunches and teas are substantial. Local crab is a speciality and of course there are Devon cream teas and Devon farm cider.

Tuna Fish Chowder

2oz (50g) butter

8oz (225g) onion, chopped

2 cloves of garlic, crushed

8oz (225g) leeks, sliced

8oz (225g) celery, sliced

8oz (225g) red and green peppers

8oz (225g) potatoes, diced

2 fish stock cubes dissolved in 1 pint (570ml) water

$\frac{1}{4}$ pint (150ml) white wine

6oz (175g) tomato purée

1lb (450g) tinned tuna fish in brine (not oil)

4oz (100g) peas (frozen)

4oz (100g) sweetcorn (frozen)

Salt and pepper

Melt the butter in a large saucepan and lightly fry the onion for 2–3 minutes with the garlic. Add the leeks, celery, peppers and potatoes and continue to cook for a further few minutes, stirring frequently. Pour in the fish stock, white wine and tomato purée and simmer gently for approximately 10–15 minutes, or until the vegetables are nearly tender. Stir in the balance of the ingredients (leaving the tuna in nice chunky pieces) and simmer for a further 10 minutes. Season to taste with salt and pepper and serve with hot crusty bread.

A meal in itself.

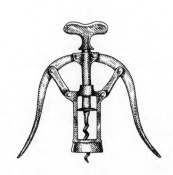

Rice Pudding

12oz (350g) long grain rice

2–2½ pints (1–1½ litres) milk

Knob of butter

4oz (100g) sugar

Pinch of salt

¼ teaspoon ground nutmeg

Small carton single or double cream

Put the rice in a heavy-bottomed saucepan. Add the milk, butter, sugar, salt and nutmeg, bring to the boil and simmer *very* gently, stirring frequently, for 30–40 minutes or until the rice is soft. If your stove is rather fierce the rice may tend to stick. Should this happen change the pan halfway through to a clean one. Just before serving, stir in the cream and pour into individual bowls. Add a swirl of jam and a dusting of nutmeg.

A very unusual method, but it works beautifully.

Nelson's Square

12oz (350g) shortcrust pastry

1 packet trifle sponge or stale cake

2 large cooking apples, coarsely grated

6oz (175g) mixed dried fruit

4oz (100g) soft brown sugar

½ level teaspoon cinnamon

½ level teaspoon mixed spice

¼ teaspoon ginger

3 eggs, beaten

Juice and rind of 1 lemon

Preheat oven: gas mark 4, 350°F, 180°C

Grease a deep-sided tin approximately 11 × 7in (28 × 18cm). If you have a food processor, process the trifle sponge or stale cake into coarse crumbs, or else use your fingers. Line the tin with two-thirds of the pastry. Cover the base with half the crumbs. Add all the grated apple and sprinkle over some of the spices. Continue with a layer of mixed fruit, then the brown sugar and sprinkle each layer with the spices. Finally, spread the balance of the crumbs evenly on top. Your tin may be quite full at this stage, but don't worry as the ingredients will sink down during cooking. Just press the whole mixture down lightly with your hand. Mix together the beaten eggs and the rind and juice of a lemon and carefully pour the liquid over the mixture as evenly as possible. Roll out the remaining pastry and place on top, sealing the edges well. If there is any pastry left over you could use it for decoration. Brush the pastry top with milk and bake in the oven for approximately 1 hour. Cool in the tin, then dust with some caster sugar or icing sugar.

This is sometimes called Drake's Square. Obviously a nautical favourite.

Saltram Fruit Cake

5oz (125g) butter or margarine	8oz (225g) mixed dried fruit
5oz (125g) caster sugar	4oz (100g) peel
2 large or 3 small eggs	2oz (50g) glacé cherries, halved
8oz (225g) self-raising flour	2oz (50g) whole or split almonds
$\frac{1}{2}$ teaspoon mixed spice	

Preheat oven: gas mark 3, 325°F, 160°C

Grease and line a 7in (18cm) round cake tin. Put the butter and sugar in a mixing bowl and beat with a wooden spoon or an electric whisk until light and fluffy. Whisk the eggs separately, then beat them into the creamed butter and sugar a little at a time. Using a large metal spoon, gently fold in the flour and mixed spice and combine. Carefully fold in the dried fruit, peel and cherries, then spoon the mixture into the prepared cake tin and smooth it out evenly with the back of the spoon. Arrange the almonds on top of the mixture. Place the cake in the centre of the oven and bake for 2–2$\frac{1}{4}$ hours, or until the centre is firm and springy to the touch. Let it cool before taking it out of the tin.

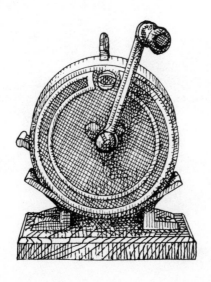

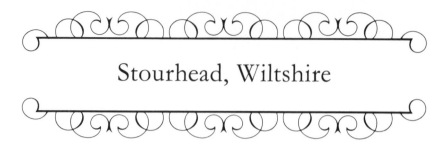

Stourhead, Wiltshire

For the wealthy and leisured classes, the 18th century was an elegant age. People had time to pursue equally elegant pastimes, and amused themselves with dancing, conversation, playing cards and walking in pleasant surroundings. The visitors to Stourhead can still enjoy a stroll in an 18th-century setting. Stourhead's 'pleasure grounds' were laid out from the 1740s by Henry Hoare II after his second wife died. He never remarried and, although he altered and improved the house and collected pictures, the gardens were his main preoccupation for the rest of his life.

Every stroll, however short, is a delight to the eye at Stourhead, but ideally you should give yourself enough time to go right round the lake to see the Grotto, the Temples of Apollo and Flora, the Cascade and all the other follies which 'Henry the Magnificent' (as Henry Hoare II was known) placed to enhance the view. The trees are awe-inspiring winter and summer alike and the garden is open all the year round. In the spring daffodils, bluebells and crocuses carpet the grassy slopes, the rhododendrons in May and June are very popular and in the autumn the foliage is breathtaking.

Stourhead House stands apart from the garden, facing the pastures and wide expanses of Salisbury Plain. It is a formal Palladian mansion redeemed from being forbiddingly plain by the lovely warm colour of its stone. Inside you can see the pictures collected by Henry and his grandson Colt Hoare and splendid original Chippendale furniture. In 1902, a disastrous fire swept the house and although most of the picture collection and furniture was happily rescued, a great deal of the house had to be reconstructed by Sir Henry, the 6th baronet, and his wife Alda, whose portraits hang in the hall.

From the car park the house is approached up a spacious drive lined by ancient chestnuts, from which the best route to the garden lies on the left. But it can also be reached down a small green valley which passes the Spread Eagle Inn, a welcoming unfussy hostelry owned by the National Trust open every day except Christmas Day, with comfortable bars and roaring fires on cold days. The excellent hot and cold buffet reflects the surroundings. The food is simple but well cooked and of high quality. There are more salads in the summer, more hot dishes in the winter, and there is always something for vegetarians. Upstairs there are four delightful bedrooms and a residents' sitting-room with a window seat. All are furnished with unsmart antiques and pretty country fabrics.

I think the recipe for a good moussaka from here is particularly appropriate. Stourhead's temples reflect the 18th-century enthusiasm for ancient Greece and Rome which was fuelled by those who went on the Grand Tour. Similarly, English cooking is now benefiting from 20th-century foreign travel!

Baked Cabbage

1 large white cabbage, shredded	$\frac{1}{4}$ teaspoon mixed spice
1 pint (570ml) white sauce	2oz (50g) grated cheese
2oz (50g) broken walnuts	2oz (50g) breadcrumbs

Preheat oven: gas mark 4, 350°F, 180°C

Cook the shredded cabbage in boiling water for 5 minutes and drain. Heat the white sauce and add the mixed spice. Put a layer of cabbage, a layer of walnuts and a layer of sauce in an ovenproof dish. Repeat in this way until the dish is full. Mix the cheese and breadcrumbs together and sprinkle on top. Place in the oven for about 25 minutes or until the top is golden and crispy.

Serve as a part of a hot buffet or as a vegetarian meal.

Red Cabbage Coleslaw

½ red cabbage, shredded
4 carrots, grated
2oz (50g) currants

5 spring onions, finely chopped
2 sticks celery, finely sliced
Mayonnaise

Mix all the prepared ingredients gently together and fold in the mayonnaise.

This is an attractive looking, quite different coleslaw which is sweeter than the usual variety.

Potatoes cooked in Stock with Oregano

1lb (450g) potatoes (use old potatoes)
¾ pint (450ml) chicken stock
2 teaspoons dried oregano, or 1 tablespoon fresh marjoram

Peel the potatoes and cut into ½in (12mm) cubes. Place in a saucepan, pour over the chicken stock and add the oregano. Bring to the boil and cook in the stock until tender but not mushy. Strain and serve.

Serve with meat or fish as an interesting winter alternative to baked or boiled potatoes.

Barbara's Moussaka

1 medium onion
Oil, vegetable or olive
1 clove garlic
1lb (450g) minced lamb
1 tablespoon tomato purée
A little white wine (optional)
Pinch of nutmeg

1lb (450g) courgettes
1 large aubergine
10oz (275g) cooked sliced potatoes
1 pint (570ml) thick cheese sauce
2oz (50g) grated Cheddar cheese

Preheat oven: gas mark 6, 400°F, 200°C

Gently cook the onion and garlic in oil for a few minutes in a large saucepan. Add the minced lamb, tomato purée, wine and nutmeg and simmer gently, preferably with a lid, until cooked. Season with salt and pepper to taste. Slice the courgettes and boil in salted water for 2 minutes, then drain well. Sprinkle the sliced aubergine with salt and leave for half an hour. Rinse the slices well to remove any excess salt and pat dry with a paper towel. Fry the slices in oil on both sides fairly slowly until soft right through and well browned. Place a layer of the cooked sliced potatoes, a layer of courgettes and aubergines and a layer of mince in an ovenproof dish. Cover well with the thick cheese sauce, sprinkle the grated cheese on top and place in the oven for 30 minutes or until the top is brown and bubbling.

Pâté-stuffed Mushrooms

20 medium-sized firm button mushrooms	1 egg
	Breadcrumbs
4oz (100g) country-style pâté	Oil to deep fry

Remove the stalks from the mushrooms and, using a teaspoon, fill the mushroom caps with the pâté, pressing it down firmly. Beat the egg until smooth. Dip the mushrooms into the egg, roll in the breadcrumbs and deep fry, a few at a time, until they are crisp and golden. Drain on kitchen paper and serve hot or cold with a garlic mayonnaise.

Serve with champagne! The French supplier of champagne to the Spread Eagle visited Mr and Mrs Willes for a tasting and it was agreed by all present that the pâté-stuffed mushrooms were the perfect accompaniment.

Treasurer's House, York

Do you believe in ghosts? If so, then the Treasurer's House is for you. Here there is not just one ghost but a full Roman legion. Harry Martindale saw them when working in the cellars thirty years ago. They appeared leading their horses and only visible from the knees up, as they were walking on the old Roman road, 18 inches below the present floor. A sad, dispirited, tired and grubby group they looked, but then York must have been an unpopular posting for a Roman soldier, cold, wet, harassed by hostile tribes and far from home.

Now this 12th-century house, surrounded by a walled garden, is part of the Minster Close. Inside, the strongest influence is that of Frank Green, Victorian industrialist and antiquary, who bought the house in 1897. He restored many of the rooms, including the Tapestry Room, the splendid Georgian Drawing-Room and the 'choose your period' Great Hall. Superficially the hall appears medieval, but in fact is part 17th-century and mostly Edwardian. The house contains some beautiful Jacobean and Georgian furniture and a fascinating clock with a 13-foot pendulum. Do look out for the studs on the floors of some of the rooms. Frank Green was such a perfectionist that he had these put in to show the servants where to place the furniture.

Leave time to see the audio-visual – the details on restoration work are very interesting – and lunch on home-made soups and other good things, or eat home-baked biscuits and cakes in the stone-walled tea-room looking out onto the garden.

Mushroom Soup

2oz (50g) butter or margarine
4oz (100g) onion
4oz (100g) leek
4oz (100g) celery
2oz (50g) flour
1 pint (570ml) chicken stock
½ pint (300ml) milk

8oz (225g) coarsely chopped mushrooms
Bouquet garni
Salt and pepper
4–5 tablespoons cream (optional)
Garnish with a few lightly fried sliced mushrooms (optional)

Slice the onion, leek and celery and gently cook them in the butter in a large, thick-bottomed saucepan without colouring. Mix in the flour and continue to cook gently. Remove from the heat, add the stock and milk and then bring to the boil, stirring frequently. Add the coarsely chopped mushrooms, bouquet garni and salt and pepper to taste and simmer for approximately 30 minutes. Remove the bouquet garni and liquidise the soup in a blender or food processor. Return to a clean pan, reheat and correct the seasoning. Just before serving stir in the cream.

Wonderful made with field mushrooms.

Lemon Mousse

3 eggs, separated
6oz (175g) caster sugar
3 large lemons

½oz (13g) gelatine
3 tablespoons water

Place the egg yolks and sugar in a mixing bowl and whisk until they become light and fluffy and the mixture has thickened. Grate the rind from 2 lemons and squeeze the juice from 3 and stir in. Place the water in a cup or small basin and sprinkle in the gelatine. Stand the cup in a saucepan of warm water and heat *very* gently until the gelatine has completely dissolved. Stir into the lemon mixture and put in a cool place. When the mixture is on the point of setting, whisk the egg whites until stiff and fold them in using a large metal spoon. Pour into individual glasses or a soufflé dish and chill. Decorate with piped cream and twists of lemon.

This is a light, refreshing and economical sweet which will also freeze very well.

Wholemeal Treacle Tart

Pastry

4oz (100g) wholemeal flour	2oz (50g) lard
4oz (100g) self-raising flour	2oz (50g) margarine
Pinch of salt	Water to bind

Filling

8oz (225g) wholemeal breadcrumbs

14 tablespoons golden syrup (if you place the tin in the oven
while it is heating up, the syrup will be easier to measure out)

Juice of $\frac{1}{2}$ lemon

Preheat oven: gas mark 5, 375°F, 190°C

First make the pastry by sifting the flours and salt into a mixing bowl
and rubbing in the fats lightly and gently with your fingertips. Sprinkle
in approximately 3 tablespoons of water at first and draw the mixture
together to form a smooth ball. If the mixture still seems crumbly and
reluctant to come together, add another tablespoon of water. If possible
rest the pastry in the fridge for 20–30 minutes before using.

Grease a 10in (25cm) flan tin, preferably using one with a loose
bottom. Roll out the pastry and line the tin. Measure out the warmed
syrup into a bowl and stir in the breadcrumbs and lemon juice. Then
pour the whole lot into the prepared pastry case. Bake in the oven for
30–35 minutes.

Pear and Ginger Loaf

8oz (225g) self-raising flour	1 ripe pear
$\frac{1}{2}$ level teaspoon ground ginger	1 egg, beaten
4oz (100g) soft brown sugar	3 tablespoons milk
4oz (100g) margarine	

Preheat oven: gas mark 4, 350°F, 180°C

Well grease a small loaf tin. Sift the flour and ginger together and then
stir in the soft brown sugar. Using your fingertips, rub in the margarine.
Peel, core and finely chop the pear and stir it into the flour mixture. Add
the beaten egg and milk and mix to a stiff dough. Turn into the loaf tin
and bake for approximately 55 minutes.

Flapjacks

2oz (50g) butter or margarine   2oz (50g) demerara sugar
4oz (100g) golden syrup   8oz (225g) rolled oats

Preheat oven: gas mark 4, 350°F, 180°C

Grease an 8in (20cm) square cake tin. Melt the butter, syrup and sugar in a saucepan. Stir in the rolled oats, turn the mixture into the cake tin and spread evenly. Bake in the oven for 30–35 minutes. Take out of the oven and cut into pieces immediately. Leave in the tin until cold.

An old favourite.

Ginger Nuts

8oz (225g) plain flour   4oz (100g) butter or margarine
½ teaspoon bicarbonate of soda   4oz (100g) caster sugar
1 teaspoon ginger   4 tablespoons golden syrup
Pinch of salt

Preheat oven: gas mark 4, 350°F, 180°C

Sift together the flour, bicarbonate of soda, ginger and salt. Melt the butter or margarine and stir in the syrup and caster sugar. Add to the dry ingredients and mix well to make a stiff dough. Roll the dough into small balls, using a teaspoon of mixture for each, and place well apart on a greased baking sheet – flatten them slightly. Bake in the oven for 15–20 minutes. Cool for a few minutes before lifting carefully from the baking sheet.

Very crisp and very economical.

Oat Biscuits

4oz (100g) margarine or butter

1 dessertspoon golden syrup

$\frac{1}{4}$ teaspoon bicarbonate of soda dissolved in 1 dessertspoon hot water

$4\frac{1}{2}$oz (113g) granulated sugar

3oz (75g) plain flour

4oz (100g) rolled oats

Preheat oven: gas mark 6, 400°F, 200°C

Grease a large baking tray. Gently melt the margarine and syrup in a saucepan. Add the bicarbonate of soda dissolved in the hot water and all the remaining ingredients. Stir with a wooden spoon until well mixed together. Place small drops on the greased baking tray, with plenty of space between each one for spreading. Bake for approximately 10 minutes.

Nutty and sustaining.

Trelissick Garden, Cornwall

Trelissick Garden lies on the banks of the River Fal in Cornwall, the last deep-water anchorage before the Atlantic Ocean. Many ships of all kinds and sizes are berthed in its creeks and estuaries. It is extraordinary to stroll in the lovely garden or the surrounding parkland, so peaceful and pastoral, with a huge oil platform, container ship or ferry looming through the trees, not 50 yards from your feet. Tam White, who runs the restaurant at Trelissick, likes to see the anchorage busy. It means the river is alive, she says, still useful, still earning its living.

Trelissick Garden was laid out amongst the hanging woods on the west side of the Fal and there are magnificent views of the river. The mild temperate climate of the south-west allows plants to flourish here which could not bear more extreme temperatures. Originally Trelissick

was a spring and early summer garden. There are wonderful displays of flowering trees, bulbs, camellias, magnolias, rhododendrons and azaleas. But now the garden is fascinating at any time. There are over a hundred kinds of hydrangea which flower until October, rare trees and autumn-colouring shrubs from China, Japan, Australia and Chile, tree ferns, unusual maples and evergreens. Trelissick is a paradise for a gardening enthusiast, but even those who know nothing about gardens will find it enchanting. There are winding woodland walks, there is always colour and scent to delight the eye and nose and throughout the garden there are wonderful views of the Fal – a reminder of England's sea-going heritage.

Two families are strongly associated with Trelissick, the Gilberts, who owned it from 1844 to 1913, and the Copelands, who inherited it in 1937. John Davies Gilbert and his son Carew Davies Gilbert planted much of the park, but the garden is the creation of Ronald and Ida Copeland. The light airy restaurant in the barn, complete with resident chaffinches and a wonderful central wood-burning stove which is full of flowers in summer, pays tribute to them both. At one end is a stone horse's head, the crest of the Copelands, while the squirrel facing it, specially carved for Trelissick, is the crest of the Gilberts.

Tam White's delicious and unusual salads are served on flower-painted Port Meirion china. Her puddings and cakes are based on traditional English recipes and her macaroons are famous – I'm lucky to have been given the recipe to share with you.

Winter Gold Soup

1lb (450g) swedes	2oz (50g) butter
1lb (450g) carrots	1½ pints (900ml) stock (using
1lb (450g) parsnips	2 stock cubes)
8oz (225g) potatoes	Salt and pepper
2 onions	Parsley to garnish

Prepare the vegetables and chop into even-sized pieces. Melt the butter in a saucepan, add all the vegetables and gently cook without browning for 10 minutes. Add the stock, cover the pan and cook for 1 hour. Cool slightly and then liquidise. Adjust the seasoning and serve hot with chopped parsley.

This makes quite a large quantity of soup, but it will keep for several days and feed a number of mouths. It also freezes well.

Carrot and Cashew Salad

1lb (450g) carrots, peeled and cut into julienne strips

4oz (100g) unsalted cashew nuts

1 small carton of plain yoghurt

Salt and pepper to taste

Mix all the ingredients together in a bowl and serve chilled.

Courgette and Red Pepper Salad

1lb (450g) courgettes, thinly sliced

1 red pepper, cut into thin strips and then diced

Vinaigrette dressing

Mix the two together in a bowl and dress with your own vinaigrette.

Green Pea and Red Kidney Bean Salad

8oz (225g) frozen petit pois

14oz (397g) tin of red kidney beans

Yoghurt, or Helmans mayonnaise, or similar

Salt and pepper

Bring the peas to the boil, then drain and run cold water over them to retain the colour. Mix the peas and beans in a bowl with either yoghurt or mayonnaise and salt and pepper to taste.

Red Cabbage, Apple and Sultana Salad

1 small red cabbage, very thinly shredded
2 apples, cored and sliced but not peeled
4oz (100g) sultanas
Vinaigrette dressing

Put all the ingredients together in a bowl and mix thoroughly. The dressing makes the salad look shiny and helps to keep the apple white.

Pork and Apricot Trelissick Pipkin

3 onions, chopped
2oz (50g) dripping
1½lb (700g) diced pork
1½oz (40g) plain flour
3 dessertspoons tomato purée
3oz (75g) dried apricots

1½ pints (900ml) stock
(you could use 2 vegetable stock cubes)
½ teaspoon mixed herbs
Salt and pepper

Preheat oven: gas mark 5, 375°F, 190°C

Fry the onions and pork in the dripping, taking care not to burn them. Stir in the flour, then add the tomato purée and stock. Place in a casserole dish with the apricots, mixed herbs, salt and pepper. Cover and cook in the oven for 1½ hours or until tender.

The pipkin in this recipe refers to the casserole dish, traditionally a pot which is glazed on the inside and coarse red earthenware on the outside.

Blackcurrant and Rum Posset

8oz (225g) blackcurrants
2oz (50g) caster sugar
¼ pint (150ml) rum

1 pint (570ml) whipping or double cream
3–4 egg whites

Place the blackcurrants and caster sugar in a saucepan and stew lightly with 2 tablespoons of water. Sieve the cooked fruit, saving a few whole blackcurrants, and add the rum. Whip the cream and fold into the blackcurrant purée. Whisk the egg whites until stiff and gently fold into the cream and fruit mixture. Spoon into individual glasses and decorate with a few of the whole fruit. Serve well chilled.

Mixed Fruit Slice

6oz (175g) dried apricot pieces
8oz (225g) dried figs
8oz (225g) stoned dates
2oz (50g) dried apple rings
Grated rind and juice of half a lemon

½ pint (300ml) water
12oz (350g) strong plain flour
6oz (175g) muesli cereal
4½oz (113g) dark brown sugar
9oz (250g) melted butter

Preheat oven: gas mark 5, 375°F, 190°C

Grease a tin approximately 10 × 7in (25 × 18cm) and line the base. Put the fruit, water, lemon rind and juice in a saucepan and simmer gently over a low heat for 7–10 minutes, stirring occasionally. Place all the remaining dry ingredients in a bowl. Melt the butter and mix thoroughly with the dry ingredients. Place half the dry mixture in the bottom of the tin, cover with the fruit mixture and then add the remaining dry mixture on top. Press down firmly. Cook in the oven for 20 minutes. Cool in the tin and slice when cold.

I am sure this fruit slice would sustain life if you had nothing else to eat.

Orange and Raisin Teabread

12oz (350g) plain flour

1½ teaspoons baking powder

¾ teaspoon bicarbonate of soda

¼ teaspoon salt

6oz (175g) brown sugar

6oz (175g) seedless raisins

Grated rind of an orange

½ pint (300ml) orange juice

1 large egg, beaten

3oz (75g) melted butter

Preheat oven: gas mark 4, 350°F, 180°C

Grease a 2lb (900g) loaf tin and line the base. Sieve flour, baking powder, bicarbonate of soda and salt into a bowl. Stir in the sugar, raisins and orange rind. Gradually beat in the orange juice with the egg and melted butter. Turn the mixture into the loaf tin and bake for 1 hour or until a knitting needle or skewer comes out clean. Cool in the tin.

Macaroons

7oz (200g) caster sugar

1oz (25g) granulated sugar

4oz (100g) ground almonds

½oz (13g) rice flour

3 egg whites

2 or 3 drops of almond essence

Rice paper and split almonds

Preheat oven: gas mark 4, 350°F, 180°C

Mix the sugars, ground almonds and rice flour together in a bowl. Add the egg whites and essence and beat everything together with a wooden spoon for about 5 minutes. Scrape down the sides of the bowl and leave to stand for 5 minutes. Meanwhile cut the rice paper into 3in (7.5cm) squares and place shiny side down on a baking sheet. Continue to beat the almond mixture for a further 5 minutes until thick and white. Using a bag and ½in (12mm) nozzle, pipe onto the rice paper – place a split almond in the centre of each macaroon and bake in the oven for 20 to 30 minutes.

Makes approximately 9.

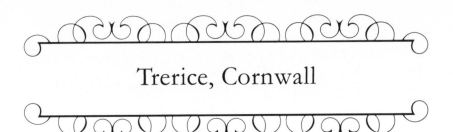

Trerice, Cornwall

To reach Trerice from the busy A38, the trunk road through Cornwall, you must twist and turn through the narrow Cornish lanes, and even then it is easy to miss, snugly buried in the beautiful Cornish countryside. Trerice was built by Sir John Arundel in 1573 in local limestone which has now weathered to a mellow silvery grey. Perhaps his service as a soldier in the Low Countries caused him to build the curving gables on the east front, unusual in the West Country and reminiscent of Amsterdam. Trerice is not a grand house, but it conveys an atmosphere of family continuity, despite the fact that it had a succession of absentee landlords in the 18th and 19th centuries. The lack of an owner on the premises meant that Trerice escaped the fate of many similar houses in Cornwall and the core of the house has not been materially altered since the late 16th century.

Inside, the Drawing-Room is the glory of the house. This is a wonderful room washed with light from the great semi-circular bay window and with rich plasterwork on the barrel ceiling and the overmantel (which displays the Arundel arms). Particularly fine plasterwork can also be seen in the Great Hall, but the plastering throughout the house is unusually splendid; even the corridors are decorated. Trerice is furnished with pictures, china and furniture associated with its history and that of the Arundel and Acland families who owned it for four centuries.

A yellow flag embroidered with a brightly-coloured Cornish chough hangs in the great barn which now houses the restaurant. It was flown at Trerice during the dark days of 1940 when invasion seemed imminent and local defence volunteers, the Home Guard, were drilled on the lawn.

Now you can sit beneath the flag, drinking the local cider and enjoying lunch or tea. What could be more pleasant than good Cornish cooking in the informal affectionate family atmosphere that is such a noticeable feature of this small delightful property?

Tomato and Rosemary Soup

8oz (225g) chopped onions

3 teaspoons chopped fresh rosemary

3 14oz (397g) tins of tomatoes (if you have fresh tomatoes use the equivalent in weight)

1 dessertspoon tomato purée

1oz (25g) sugar

1½ pints (900ml) chicken stock

1 heaped tablespoon cornflour

½ pint (300ml) single cream

Salt and pepper

Parsley to garnish

Place the chopped onions, rosemary, tomatoes, tomato purée, sugar and stock in a large saucepan. Reserve a little of the stock to cream the cornflour. Add the blended cornflour to the pan and simmer all the ingredients for approximately 20 minutes. Remove from the heat and liquidise. Adjust the seasoning. Reheat and stir in the cream just before serving. Serve very hot with a garnish of chopped parsley.

A very economical soup recipe, but special enough for a dinner party.

Brown Rice and Cheese Salad

12oz (350g) brown rice

6oz (175g) mature Cheddar cheese, cubed

2oz (50g) sultanas

2oz (50g) toasted flaked almonds

A bunch of spring onions, chopped

Vinaigrette to taste

Cook the brown rice and cool. Add all the other ingredients and mix well. Serve with either a tomato salad or a green salad. It looks lovely served on a bed of lettuce as a light vegetarian meal.

Fennel and Cabbage Salad

1½lb (700g) white cabbage

1 tablespoon fennel seeds

3 medium oranges, peeled and chopped

Vinaigrette using lemon juice instead of vinegar

Fresh parsley (a good handful)

Shred the cabbage and add all the other ingredients. Mix gently and serve.

Lemon Meringue Pie

Crust
8oz (225g) shortcrust pastry

Filling

½ pint (300ml) water

2½oz (65g) cornflour

6oz (175g) sugar

Grated rind and juice of 3 lemons

3 egg yolks

1oz (25g) butter

Topping
3 egg whites

6oz (175g) sugar

Preheat oven: gas mark 5, 375°F, 190°C

Grease a 7½in (19cm) flan tin and line with shortcrust pastry. Prick the base with a fork and bake in the oven for 20–25 minutes or until cooked. Remove the pastry case from the oven and immediately lower the heat to gas mark 2, 300°F, 150°C for the meringue.

Cream the cornflour to a paste with a little of the water in a bowl and add the sugar. Pour the rest of the water and the grated lemon rind into a saucepan and bring to the boil. Pour onto the cornflour and sugar paste and mix until smooth. Transfer the mixture back to the saucepan and bring back to the boil. Simmer gently for 1 minute, stirring all the time to prevent it from catching. Remove the pan from the heat and beat in the egg yolks, lemon juice and butter. Pour the lemon mixture into the pastry case and spread it out evenly.

Whisk the egg whites until stiff. Beat in a quarter of the sugar at a time until it is all incorporated, then spread the meringue mixture all over the filling. Cook for 45 minutes and serve hot or cold.

Chocolate Cake

10oz (275g) self-raising flour
½ teaspoon salt
1¼oz (35g) cocoa
6oz (175g) caster sugar
5oz (125g) margarine

7oz (200g) golden syrup
½ pint (300ml) milk
1 teaspoon bicarbonate of soda
½ teaspoon vanilla essence

Preheat oven: gas mark 4, 350°F, 180°C

Grease and line an 8in (20cm) round cake tin. Sieve the flour, salt, cocoa, and bicarbonate of soda in a large bowl and then add the caster sugar. Melt the margarine and syrup in a saucepan and pour in the milk and vanilla essence. Add the liquid to the dry ingredients very gradually, beating with a rotary whisk to remove any lumps. Spoon into the baking tin and bake for 1–1¼ hours. Split and sandwich with a coffee butter cream filling when cold.

Very easy and very rewarding to cook.

Date and Walnut Loaf

4oz (100g) margarine
1lb (450g) dates
4oz (100g) sugar
Pinch of salt
2 teaspoons bicarbonate of soda

½ pint (300ml) boiling water
4oz (100g) walnuts
2 eggs, beaten
1lb (450g) self-raising flour

Preheat oven: gas mark 3, 325°F, 160°C

Grease a 2lb (900g) loaf tin and line the base. Put the margarine, dates, sugar, salt and bicarbonate of soda into a large mixing bowl. Pour over the boiling water and allow to cool. Add the walnuts, eggs and flour and mix until well combined. Spoon into the loaf tin and bake for 1–1¼ hours.

A big loaf which keeps well; best eaten buttered.

Shortbread

4oz (100g) butter or margarine (at room temperature)

2oz (50g) caster sugar

6oz (175g) plain flour

Preheat oven: gas mark 2, 300°F, 150°C

Well grease a 7½in (19cm) flan tin. Beat the butter in a bowl until soft, then beat in the sugar followed by the flour. Work all the ingredients together using a wooden spoon, then gather the mixture into a ball with your hands. Press the mixture evenly into the tin with your hands, and flute the edges with your fingers. Prick the shortbread all over with a fork and bake for about 45 minutes. While still warm, use a palette knife to mark out the surface in wedges. Cool in the tin, turn out and dust with caster sugar.

Scones

8oz (225g) self-raising flour

1½oz (40g) margarine or butter (at room temperature)

2oz (50g) sugar

Pinch of salt

¼ pint (150ml) milk

Preheat oven: gas mark 8, 450°F, 220°C

Rub the flour and fat together in a bowl using your fingertips until the mixture resembles fine breadcrumbs. Stir in the sugar and salt. Pour in enough milk to give a fairly soft dough. Knead lightly with your hands and place the dough onto a floured pastry board. Roll out to a thickness of not less than ¾in (2cm). Cut into 10–12 rounds using a 2in (5cm) cutter and place the scones on a greased baking sheet. Dust with a little extra flour or brush with beaten egg or milk and bake near the top of the oven for 8–10 minutes.

Wordsworth House, Cumbria

Cockermouth lies in countryside which recalls an early Victorian water-colour. Hillsides, lakes and trees are bathed in a misty light, a fitful sun illuminates small whitewashed and stone cottages, sheep graze peace-fully and there is a glimpse of a higher peak. It seems entirely appropriate that in 1770 this was the birthplace of that unpretentious genius William Wordsworth, poet laureate and a leading figure of the Romantic movement.

Wordsworth House is a pretty peach-washed Georgian house on the High Street. John, William's father, lived here in some style as lawyer and agent to Sir John Lowther, the local tycoon and landowner. It came to the Trust empty and has been furnished with immense care to convey the atmosphere of a prosperous middle-class Georgian household. The dining-room and drawing-rooms were for entertaining, only used when guests were present. The prints and paintings on the original panelled walls are hung from rosettes on copper wire in the 18th-century manner. The table in the dining-room is laid for dessert, with authentic wax fruits on the raised glass dish and caraway and pepper biscuits made to original 18th-century 'receipts'. Tea is laid out in the parlour where the family would have sat. The spinning wheel, writing materials and books here are all of the period. Throughout the house, the bare floor boards are scrubbed with sand in the original fashion.

Upstairs there are a bookcase and a desk owned by the poet, candle-sticks which Dorothy Wordsworth, his sister, gave to friends as a wedding present and the poet's inkstand. There is an exhibition of pictures, photographs of the Cockermouth Wordsworth might have known and a slide show accompanied by readings from his poems. It is impossible not to feel closer to the man and the poet after visiting the house.

The restaurant here is unique. Your food is cooked in the old kitchen, and then served in the housekeeper's room by mob-capped frilly-aproned ladies. If the weather is cold, the range is lit and crackles welcomingly. A collection of willow-pattern china gleams against the wall. Recipes have a distinctive local flavour. The port of Whitehaven, on the nearby Cumbrian coast, conducted a thriving trade with the West Indies in the 18th century, importing rum, dried fruits and spices. Local housewives used these delicacies to create 'receipts' which are now traditional Cumberland fare. Buttermere fudge cake, Cumberland spiced butter and matrimonial tart are all on the menu here. Some of the recipes are given below, but I heartily recommend visiting Wordsworth House to taste for yourself.

Savoury Herb Potted Cheese

5oz (125g) Stilton cheese
5oz (125g) Cheddar cheese
1 dessertspoon mixed herbs

Single cream
(about a small carton – $\frac{1}{4}$ pint (150ml))

Finely grate the Stilton and Cheddar cheese. Beat in the mixed herbs together with enough single cream to give a smooth paste – a food processor can be used to make a very smooth paste. Pack into four individual pots garnished with parsley.

Serve with savoury shortbread, toast or herb scones as a snack or light lunch.

Border Tart

8oz (225g) shortcrust pastry

6oz (175g) currants

2oz (50g) walnuts, chopped lightly

2oz (50g) butter

2oz (50g) brown sugar

1 egg

Icing

3oz (75g) icing sugar

Lemon juice

Preheat oven: gas mark 6, 400°F, 200°C

Grease and line an 8in (20cm) flan tin with the pastry. Wash the currants and put in a saucepan with the walnuts, butter and sugar. Melt gently, stirring all the time, then turn the mixture into the flan case and spread evenly all over the base. Beat the egg well and pour over the flan filling. Bake in the oven for 25–30 minutes until set, then take the tart out and leave to cool. In the meantime mix the icing sugar with enough lemon juice to make a pouring water icing. Dribble this over the flan filling and leave to set.

Cumberland Spiced Butter

8oz (225g) soft brown sugar

5oz (125g) unsalted butter

1 teaspoon ground cinnamon

$\frac{1}{4}$ teaspoon nutmeg

$\frac{1}{4}$ teaspoon mixed spice

With a wooden spoon, or better still an electric whisk, cream together the butter and sugar until soft and creamy. Add the spices and beat in. Serve in pots and use to spread on hot scones or toasted teacakes. Will keep at least a month in a fridge if well wrapped.

This is also delicious with Christmas pudding.

Ginger Almond Tart

8oz (225g) shortcrust pastry

4 tablespoons ginger preserve

3oz (75g) light brown sugar

3oz (75g) butter or margarine

2 eggs

$\frac{1}{2}$ teaspoon almond essence

2oz (50g) soya flour
(obtainable from health food
shops)

$\frac{1}{2}$ teaspoon baking powder

Icing

2oz (50g) icing sugar

Water to mix

Almond essence

Flaked almonds (optional)

Preheat oven: gas mark 3, 325°F, 160°C

Line an 8in (20cm) flan tin with the shortcrust pastry. Spread the base with the chopped ginger preserve. Cream the sugar and butter in a bowl until light and fluffy. Gradually beat in the eggs, one at a time – should the mixture curdle at this stage add 1 teaspoon of soya flour which should correct this. Add the almond essence, soya flour and baking powder and mix until well combined. Spread this over the ginger preserve right to the edge of the flan and bake in the oven for approximately 1 hour until risen and golden. Leave to cool.

Spread the top with glacé icing made with the icing sugar, water and almond essence to flavour and leave to set. If you wish you can sprinkle the top with flaked almonds to decorate.

For those with a sweet tooth – delicious and very rich.

LOCAL STOCKISTS

National Trust restaurants serve a variety of products, often locally produced, which visitors might like to purchase themselves for home consumption. Local stockists for some of these items are given below.

Apple juice

Copella Apple Juice as served in many restaurants can be bought from good grocery shops or health food shops all over England.

Cheese (as served at Killerton)

The farmhouse cheeses produced by J. G. Quicke & Partners can by obtained from The Farm Shop, Home Farm, Newton St Cyres.

(as served at Baddesley Clinton)

The Cheddars produced by Fowlers Forest Dairies Ltd can be obtained in a number of shops in the East Midlands including:

The Cardinal, Station Road, Solihull, Warwicks.

Sampsons, Lapworth, Warwicks.

Eric Lyons, Knowle, Warwicks.

Devlins, Kenilworth, Warwicks.

Clotted cream (as served at Saltram)

The cream is made in Plymouth by the Devon Co-operative Society and is widely available from co-op grocery shops in most Devon towns.

Game pie (as served at Hidcote)

The pies, together with home-made sausages and other products, are made by H. H. Collins and sold in their own shop at 28 North Street, Broadway, Worcestershire.

Ice-cream (as served at Killerton, Knightshayes and Saltram)

This is Salcombe dairy ice-cream which is available from:

Harlequin's Ice-cream Parlour, Queen Street, Exeter, Devon

Crebers, Brook Street, Tavistock, Devon

Country Cupboard, Bampton Street, Tiverton, Devon

Pâtés (as served at Killerton, Knightshayes and Saltram)

These are made by the Budleigh Pâté Company and are available at good delicatessens throughout Devon.

Teas

The teas served in National Trust restaurants are specially selected for the National Trust and can be bought from the National Trust shops at the properties.

Wine

Lamberhurst English wines are served in many of the restaurants and are available from most good off-licences throughout England.

The wine served at Anglesey Abbey is made by Chilford Hall and available from the vineyard at Chilford Hall, Balsham Road, Linton, Cambridge. They welcome visitors and organise tours of the vineyard.

The wine served at Knightshayes Court is made by Highfields Vineyards and is available from the vineyard at Longdrag, Tiverton, Devon. They also welcome visitors, organise tours of the vineyard and produce a delicious mustard which can be bought from the National Trust shop at Knightshayes.

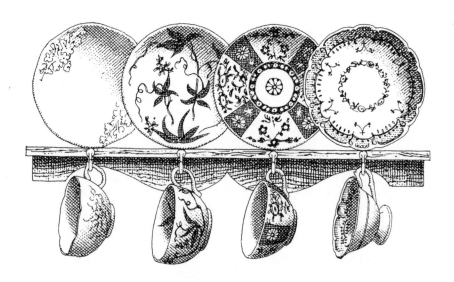

NATIONAL TRUST RESTAURANTS

AVON

Dyrham Park
Unlicensed tea-room
The Orangery, Dyrham Park,
Chippenham
Tel: (027582) 2501

BERKSHIRE

Basildon Park
Unlicensed tea-room
Lower Basildon, Reading
Tel: (07357) 3040

Cliveden
Unlicensed restaurant
Taplow, Maidenhead
Tel: (06286) 61406

BUCKINGHAMSHIRE

Claydon House
Unlicensed tea-room
Middle Claydon, Nr Buckingham
Tel: (029673) 349 or 693

Hughenden Manor
Unlicensed tea-room
High Wycombe
Tel: (0494) 32580

CAMBRIDGESHIRE

Anglesey Abbey
Licensed restaurant
Lode, Cambridge
Tel: (0223) 811200

Peckover House
Unlicensed tea-room
North Brink, Wisbech
Tel: (0945) 583463

Wimpole Hall
Licensed restaurant

Wimpole Home Farm House
Unlicensed refreshments
Arrington, Nr Royston,
Hertfordshire
Tel: (0223) 207257

CHESHIRE

Dunham Massey
Licensed restaurant
Altrincham
Tel: (061941) 1025

Little Moreton Hall
Unlicensed tea-room
Congleton
Tel: (0260) 272018

CLEVELAND

Ormesby Hall
Light refreshments
Ormesby, Middlesbrough
Tel: (0642) 324188

CORNWALL

Bedruthan Steps
Unlicensed café
St Eval, Wadebridge
Tel: (0637) 860563

Cotehele
Licensed restaurant
St Dominick, Saltash
Tel: (0579) 50652

Unlicensed restaurant
The Edgcumbe Arms
The Quay, Cotehele,
St Dominick
Tel: (0579) 50024

Lanhydrock
Licensed restaurant
Lanhydrock Park, Bodmin
Tel: (0208) 4331

St Michael's Mount
Licensed restaurant
The Sail Loft Restaurant
St Michael's Mount, Marazion,
Penzance
Tel: (0736) 710748

Trelissick Garden
Licensed restaurant
Feock, Truro
Tel: (0872) 863486

Trerice
Licensed restaurant
St Newlyn East, Newquay
Tel: (0637) 875404

CUMBRIA

Fell Foot
Unlicensed café
Fell Foot Park, Newby Bridge,
Ulverston
Tel: (053 95) 31273

Sizergh Castle
Unlicensed tea-room
Nr Kendal
Tel: (05395) 60070

Wordsworth House
Licensed restaurant
Main Street, Cockermouth
Tel: (0900) 824805

DERBYSHIRE

Hardwick Hall
Licensed restaurant
Doe Lea, Chesterfield
Tel: (0246) 850430

Kedleston Hall
Licensed restaurant
Kedleston, Derby
Tel: (0332) 842191

Longshaw Lodge
Unlicensed café
Longshaw, Sheffield
Tel: (0433) 31708

Sudbury Hall
Unlicensed restaurant
Sudbury Coach House, Sudbury
Tel: (028378) 597

DEVON

Arlington Court
Licensed restaurant
Arlington, Nr Barnstaple
Tel: (027 182) 348

Castle Drogo
Licensed restaurant
Drewsteignton, Exeter
Tel: (06473) 3306

Killerton
Licensed restaurant
Broadclyst, Exeter
Tel: (0392) 881345

Knightshayes Court
Licensed restaurant
Bolham, Tiverton
Tel: (0884) 254665

Saltram
Licensed restaurant
Plympton, Plymouth
Tel: (0752) 336546

Watersmeet House
Unlicensed tea-room
Lynmouth
Tel: (0598) 3348

DORSET

Brownsea Island
Licensed café
Café Villano, Brownsea Island,
Poole Harbour
Tel: (0202) 700244

Corfe Castle
Licensed tea-room
Castle Tea-room, Corfe Castle,
Nr Wareham
Tel: (0929) 480921

Kingston Lacy
Unlicensed restaurant
Wimborne Minster
Tel: (0202) 883402

EAST SUSSEX

Bateman's
Licensed tea-room
Burwash, Etchingham
Tel: (0435) 882302

Bodiam Castle
Licensed café
Bodiam, Nr Robertsbridge
Tel: (058083) 436

GLOUCESTERSHIRE

Hidcote Manor Garden
Licensed tea-room
Hidcote, Bartrim,
Chipping Campden
Tel: (038677) 703

HAMPSHIRE

The Vyne
Unlicensed tea-room
Sherborne St John, Basingstoke
Tel: (0256) 881337

HEREFORD & WORCESTER

Berrington Hall
Unlicensed tea-room
Leominster
Tel: (0568) 5721

Hanbury Hall
Unlicensed tea-room
Droitwich
Tel: (052784) 214

KENT

Chartwell
Licensed restaurant
Westerham
Tel: (0732) 866368

Sissinghurst Castle
Licensed tea-room
Sissinghurst, Cranbrook
Tel: (0580) 713097

LANCASHIRE

Rufford Old Hall
Unlicensed tea-room
Rufford, Nr Ormskirk
Tel: (0704) 821254

LINCOLNSHIRE

Belton House
Licensed restaurant
Nr Grantham
Tel: (0476) 66116

MERSEYSIDE

Speke Hall
Unlicensed tea-room
Liverpool
Tel: (051427) 7231

NORFOLK

Blickling Hall
Licensed restaurant
Blickling, Norwich
Tel: (0263) 733084

Felbrigg Hall
Licensed restaurant
Felbrigg, Norwich
Tel: (026375) 444

Oxburgh Hall
Unlicensed tea-room
Oxborough, Kings Lynn
Tel: (36621) 258

NORTHANTS

Canons Ashby
Unlicensed tea-room
Daventry
Tel: (0327) 860044

NORTHERN IRELAND

The Argory (Co. Armagh)
Light refreshments
Moy, Dungannon, Co. Tyrone
Tel: (08687) 84753

Castle Ward
Unlicensed tea-room
Strangford, Downpatrick,
Co. Down
Tel: (039686) 204

Florence Court
Unlicensed tea-room
Nr Enniskillen, Co. Fermanagh
Tel: (036582) 249

Giant's Causeway
Unlicensed tea-room
Bushmills, Co. Antrim
Tel: (02657) 31582

Mount Stewart
Unlicensed tea-room
Newtownards, Co. Down
Tel: (024744) 387

NORTHUMBERLAND

Cragside
Licensed restaurant
Rothbury, Morpeth
Tel: (0669) 20134

Housesteads
Light refreshments
Bardon Mill, Hexham
Tel: (04984) 525

Wallington
Unlicensed restaurant
The Clock Tower Restaurant,
Wallington, Cambo, Morpeth
Tel: (067074) 274

NORTH YORKSHIRE

Beningbrough Hall
Licensed restaurant
Shipton-by-Beningbrough, York
Tel: (0904) 470715

Brimham Rocks
Unlicensed kiosk
Summerbridge, Nr Harrogate
Tel: (0423) 780688

Fountains Abbey & Studley Royal
Licensed restaurant
Studley Royal Park, Nr Ripon
Tel: (0765) 4246

Nunnington Hall
Unlicensed tea-room
Nunnington, York
Tel: (04395) 283

Treasurer's House
Licensed tea-room
Minster Yard, York
Tel: (0904) 646757

NOTTINGHAMSHIRE

Clumber Park
Unlicensed tea-room
Worksop
Tel: (0909) 484122

OXFORDSHIRE

Greys Court
Unlicensed tea-room
Rotherfield Greys,
Nr Henley-on-Thames
Tel: (04917) 529

SHROPSHIRE

Attingham Park
Unlicensed tea-room
Shrewsbury
Tel: (074377) 203

Carding Mill Valley
Unlicensed café
Chalet Pavilion, Church Stretton
Tel: (0694) 722631

Dudmaston
Unlicensed tea-room
Quatt, Bridgnorth
Tel: (0746) 780866

SOMERSET

Montacute House
Licensed café
Nr Yeovil
Tel: (0935) 824575

STAFFORDSHIRE

Moseley Old Hall
Unlicensed tea-room
Fordhouses, Wolverhampton
Tel: (0902) 782808

SUFFOLK

Flatford
Unlicensed café
Bridge Cottage, Flatford,
East Bergholt, Colchester
Tel: (0206) 298260

Ickworth
Licensed restaurant
Horringer, Bury St Edmunds
Tel: (028488) 270

Lavenham
Unlicensed tea-room
The Guildhall, Market Place,
Lavenham
Tel: (0787) 247646

SURREY

Box Hill
Licensed restaurant
Tadworth
Tel: (0306) 888793

Clandon Park
Licensed restaurant
West Clandon, Guildford
Tel: (0483) 222502

Claremont
Light refreshments
Portsmouth Road, Esher

Hatchlands
Unlicensed tea-room
East Clandon, Guildford
Tel: (0483) 222787

Polesden Lacey
Licensed restaurant
Nr Dorking
Tel: (0372) 56190

WALES

Chirk Castle
Licensed tea-room
Chirk, Clywd
Tel: (0691) 777701

Erddig
Licensed tea-room
Wrexham, Clwyd
Tel: (0978) 355314

Penrhyn Castle
Licensed tea-room
Bangor, Gwynedd
Tel: (0248) 353084

Plas Newydd
Licensed tea-room
Llanfairpwll, Isle of Anglesey,
Gwynedd
Tel: (0248) 714795

Powis Castle
Licensed tea-room
Welshpool, Powys
Tel: (0938) 5499

WARWICKSHIRE

Baddesley Clinton
Licensed tea-room
Knowle, Solihull
Tel: (05643) 3294

Charlecote Park
Unlicensed tea-room
Wellesbourne, Warwick
Tel: (0789) 840277

Coughton Court
Unlicensed tea-room
Alcester
Tel: (0789) 762435

WEST SUSSEX

Nymans Garden
Light refreshments
Handcross, Nr Haywards Heath
Tel: (0444) 400002

Petworth House
Unlicensed tea-room
Petworth
Tel: (0798) 42207

Standen
Unlicensed tea-room
East Grinstead
Tel: (0342) 23029

Uppark
Unlicensed tea-room
South Harting, Petersfield
Tel: (073085) 317

WEST YORKSHIRE

East Riddlesden Hall
Unlicensed tea-room
Bradford Road, Keighley
Tel: (0535) 607075

WILTSHIRE

Stourhead
Licensed inn
The Spread Eagle Inn, Stourton,
Nr Warminster
Tel: (0747) 840587

Stourton Village Hall
Unlicensed tea-room
Stourton, Nr Warminster

AMERICAN EQUIVALENTS

Dry Measures

1 US cup = 50g = 2oz of: breadcrumbs; fresh cake crumbs

1 US cup = 75g = 3oz of: rolled oats

1 US cup = 90g = $3\frac{1}{2}$oz of: desiccated coconut; ground almonds

1 US cup = 100g = 4oz of: suet; grated hard cheese; walnut pieces; drinking chocolate; icing sugar; cocoa; flaked almonds; pasta; frozen peas

1 US cup = 125g = 5oz of: white flour; self-raising flour; currants; muesli; chopped dates; ground roasted almonds

1 US cup = 150g = $5\frac{1}{2}$oz of: wholemeal flour; raisins; cornflour

1 US cup = 175g = 6oz of: apricots; mixed peel; sultanas

1 US cup = 200g = 7oz of: caster sugar; soft brown sugar; demerara sugar; glacé cherries; lentils; long grain and brown rice; flaked and drained tuna fish

1 US cup = 225g = $\frac{1}{2}$lb of: cream cheese; cottage cheese

1 US cup = 300g = 11oz of: mincemeat; marmalade

1 US cup = 350g = 12oz of: syrup; treacle; jam

Liquid Measures

$\frac{1}{4}$ US cup = 60ml = 2 fluid oz
1 US cup = 240ml = 8 fluid oz
2 US cups (1 US pint) = 480ml = 16 fluid oz

Butter, Lard and Margarine Measures

$\frac{1}{4}$ stick = 25g = 2 level tablespoons = 1oz
1 stick ($\frac{1}{2}$ US cup) = 100g = 8 level tablespoons = 4oz

Information very kindly provided by the Good Housekeeping Institute

INDEX